THE
VICTOR
SPEAKS

EDMUND SCHLINK

THE
VICTOR
SPEAKS

Translated by

PAUL F. KOEHNEKE

CONCORDIA PUBLISHING HOUSE · SAINT LOUIS

The Victor Speaks, translated by permission, was
first published under the title *Der Erhöhte spricht*
by the Furche-Verlag, Hamburg

PREFACE

CONCORDIA PUBLISHING HOUSE had commissioned the Reverend Professor Paul F. Koehneke, D. D., of Milwaukee, Wisconsin, to translate Prof. Edmund Schlink's *Der Erhöhte spricht* (THE VICTOR SPEAKS). His task was not completed when the Victor summoned him to the glory of heaven on Ash Wednesday, 1956.

The unfinished task was assumed by the undersigned, his son, and by Professor Daniel E. Poellot, both of Concordia Teachers College, River Forest, Illinois.

The translation is dedicated to the memory of my sainted father, who was persuaded of the worth of THE VICTOR SPEAKS for English readers.

The author speaks at times in ways which force translators to make a choice. One must either be completely faithful in translation or alter the translation to suit a stranslator's point of view. We have chosen the former course, and have left the results to the critical judgment of the reader.

Professor Schlink has been teaching at the University of Heidelberg, Germany, since 1946 and has been one of the prominent Lutheran leaders in the affairs of the church. Some of his major writings are:

Der Mensch in der Verkündigung der Kirche (1935),
Theologie der luther. Bekenntnisschriften (1940, 3d ed.
1948), and *Der Ertrag des Kirchenkampfes* (1947).

May THE VICTOR SPEAKS serve as a means toward
greater victories for the victorious Christ!

M. L. KOEHNEKE

CONTENTS

Introduction

EVEN in His deepest humiliation Jesus Christ is the exalted Savior. According to the testimony of John's Gospel His crucifixion was His exaltation. The Crucified is lifted up, helplessly hanging and dying on the tree between heaven and earth. But His hanging on the cross, His defeat, is His victory. Through it He established His royal rule over all sinners.

On the other hand, Scripture usually speaks of His exaltation as the rising of the crucified Jesus from the grave to the right hand of His Father, whence He rules over everything and whence He shall come to judge the quick and the dead. This speedy return of the risen Lord to the Father again is full of humiliation and condescension. Raised from the dead, He immediately returns humbly yet royally to the despairing fools who once were His disciples.

May we come to be entirely certain of this oneness of the crucified and risen Lord! God grant that we see clearly the exaltation of the crucified Savior and the humiliation of the exalted Savior. Then we, too, are victors in defeat — "as dying, and, behold, we live; as chastened and not killed; as sorrowful, yet always rejoicing; as poor, yet making many rich; as having nothing, and yet possessing all things." (2 Cor. 6:9 f.)

CHAPTER I

The First Word on the Cross

And when they were come to the place which is called Calvary, there they crucified Him, and the malefactors, one on the right hand and the other on the left. Then said Jesus: Father, forgive them; for they know not what they do. And they parted His raiment and cast lots. (Luke 23:33,34)

DO NOT LOOK for the cross of Christ in Palestine alone. See it right among us! Do not look for the cross of Christ in the past alone, in the year of our Lord 30. See it in the present, it is standing among us! The black sky brooding over Golgotha is arched above us too. The tempest and the earthquake which terrified Jerusalem terrify us also. Do not envision the cross of Christ as something far away. It is as near and contemporary as anything can be. Even though it is certain that Christ died only once, in the year 30, on Calvary's hill, so far away, and will never die again, it is just as certain that He has not ceased to suffer with mankind. There is no human distress which He does not share. There is no human despair which He, too, does not feel. For when hunger torments one of us He says, "I am hungry." When one of us suffers thirst He says, "I am thirsty." There is no nakedness of which Christ does not say, "I am naked"; no sickness, of which He does not say, "I am sick" (Matt. 25:35 ff.). Thus Christ's suffering and human suffering go on together through the ages. And the crucified Lord comes to us in the sorrow that is ours and in the suffering that is our neighbor's.

The cross of Christ stands among us — in our nation, in our city, in our calling. No one can say that he is not standing under the cross of Christ. If it is terrible that Christ's suffering has not yet come to an end, it is inconceivably gruesome that those for whom He died on Calvary are the very ones who are still crucifying Him. For He does not merely say, "Your misery is My misery, your cross is My own cross," but He also says, "Inasmuch as ye did it not to one of the least of these, ye did it not to Me." Do not look for the crucifiers in Palestine alone. See them among us! Do not see them only in the Jews and Romans of the year 30. Discover them also among us. Just as the cross of Christ stands among us, so also there stand among us those who still torment, ridicule, taunt, and crucify Him.

But the crucifiers are not only among us — we are the crucifiers! We crucify Christ if we do not hunger with those who hunger and do not mourn

4

with those who mourn. We crucify Christ when we leave a desperate person to his despair, and abandon the insolent man to the loneliness of his insolence. We crucify Him when we either smugly or timidly shun our fellow man. We crucify Him when out of a false moral sense or an inflated notion of our dignity we "let our brother down" in his misery. We raise the cross of Christ again and again when we rebel against our own suffering and curse God, who by this very suffering desires to unite us with Christ, yes, even clothe us with Him. We extend the suffering of Christ when we do not see in our own suffering the cross of Christ, do not take it upon us and love it. We crucify Christ by being secure when we should tremble and by being fearful when we should believe. We are the ones who are crucifying Christ anew.

As then, the cross of Christ is raised up today, and as they did then, men crucify Christ today. Now, is the first word of Christ on the cross as valid today as it was then?

When Jesus was reviled, He reviled not again. He knew everyone who had ridiculed and beaten Him and nailed Him to the cross. But on the cross He did not address a single one of them. He answered His crucifiers with silence. He did not call down to them, but called to the very God whose majesty was being outraged and whose mercy was being rejected. He turned to Him who had the power to send legions

5

of angels and to put an end to the cruelty of the cross and the blasphemy of the crucifiers.

But this is what He cried to God: Forget your majesty and holiness, forget your power and honor — and forgive! Forget the crime that is being committed here! He did not turn to God the Judge, but simply to the Father. He did not utter a psalm of innocence, to swear that He had not deserved the cross. Nor did He utter a psalm of vengeance to demand victory for God's righteousness by punishing the crucifiers, and victory for His honor by setting Him free. He called for mercy rather than holiness. There was no appeal to divine majesty, which in view of the monstrous blasphemy discharging itself in the crucifixion would have had to pierce the black sky like a bolt of lightning to put an end to the blasphemy. Nor did Jesus ask to be freed from the cross or to be vindicated before men, much less to have His suffering shortened. He had only one desire: the dreadful sin of His enemies was to be sin no more.

However, Jesus not only prayed for forgiveness for His murderers but also let them know that He prayed for them. He had kept silence before His crucifiers. He now broke His silence by crying aloud in prayer so that those standing about could hear Him. He who had taught His disciples to pray in the closet humbled Himself so deeply before His murderers that He prayed openly before men and not in the quiet chamber of His heart. He was mindful of the fact that forgiveness is of no value if forgiveness is not known, and He did not want His murderers to be without comfort if after Easter they realized and knew whom they had killed. Here a gift of incomprehensible love and goodness is brilliantly displayed and lets the present with all its sin be gone. Jesus comforted His murderers in advance, even though they did not at all understand His prayer — "for they know not what they do."

Does this prayer of Christ Crucified apply also to us who in this twentieth century stand about His cross and renew His agonies?

The executioners who pressed the body of Christ on the cross and fastened it there did not know whom they were crucifying. The Romans among them saw only one of the many religious controversies involving only the Jews, and in their opinion these quarrels had no significance for them. The Jews among them saw only one of the many false messiahs who appeared from time to time and stirred up the people. Since the days of their childhood their teachers and religious leaders had presented the true Messiah to them in an altogether different light. When the Romans heard someone talk of the son of god, they thought of the emperor. When the Jews spoke of the Messiah, they thought of their future hero and national liberator. For none of them Jesus was an outstanding or special person, but only one of the many, all too many, superfluous persons. Why should He in any way impress them when they were nailing Him to the cross? For they had not yet perceived the obedience revealed in His dying. Nor had they heard the words that He spoke in His dying hours. Above all, they all, the scribes and elders included, did not know that the Crucified would miraculously rise again after three days and, exalted by God, would have an eternal future. They knew not what they did.

Our situation is different. We can know that neither a national hero nor an emperor will help us, and we need not be shocked because Jesus fulfilled neither Roman nor Jewish political expectations. For we have been told that Jesus did not remain in the grave, but rose again and overcame death. As a result all false political hopes are condemned. We are not living before Easter, as did the Jews and Romans on Golgotha, but we have known from childhood that the Crucified revealed Himself as Victor and has been exalted to be the Lord of the world, sitting at the right hand of God. Consequently there stands for us a tremendous exclamation mark behind the cross of Jesus, a mark which distinguishes this criminal from all others, this cross from every other cross. By means of it, in spite of the highly compressed record, we are told infinitely more about Jesus than all His murderers knew, to say nothing of the many witnesses and signs by which Jesus since His exaltation again and again proved Himself to be the Lord. This exclamation mark the executioners on Golgotha did not see! But can *we* still say that *we* know not what we do? Is it still true that by our lovelessness, smugness, and fear, we revile, beat, and crucify the Christ whom we do not know? Rather isn't this the case, that we know very well what we are doing when, instead of beginning a new life in the power of His death, we again and again torment the Christ who died for us?

Both the past of Golgotha and our modern day have the raised cross of the Lord in common. The present and the past have the crucifiers in common, since we, too, crucify Him. But does the similarity come to an end when we look at the Lord's argument for His plea for forgiveness? Is it therefore possible that Jesus' prayer "Father, forgive them" is valid for the murderers of the year 30, but not for us, the crucifiers of the twentieth century, because we do know what we do? Is this prayer, with its singular argument "for they know not what they do," possibly valid and effective for every ungodly person and pagan, indeed, for any human being, except for Christians?

Let no one evade this question! It is intended to deeply penetrate like a barb and to inflict a painful wound in us. This wound is not to heal at once, but must remain open. The barb dare not be removed at once, but must continue to stick in the wound and torment us. Only with this wound in our heart shall we understand the Passion of the Lord. Only he who has been wounded is healed by the cross.

CHAPTER II

The Second Word on the Cross

*And one of the malefactors which were hanged railed on Him,
saying, If Thou be Christ, save Thyself and us. But the other
answering rebuked him, saying, Dost not thou fear God,
seeing thou art in the same condemnation? And we indeed
justly; for we receive the due reward of our deeds; but this
Man hath done nothing amiss. And he said unto Jesus, Lord,
remember me when Thou comest into Thy kingdom. And
Jesus said unto him, Verily I say unto thee, today shalt thou
be with Me in Paradise.* (Luke 23:39-43)

JESUS HUNG on the cross not to eternalize man's sin
but to put an end to it. He suffered not to increase
man's misery but to remove it. He suffered not to
perpetuate our despair over the vanity and futility of
all that is noble and good (since God Himself here
did not refuse to submit to the law of destruction)
but to snatch man from inevitable self-destruction.
He did not intend to move us to sympathetic tears
at the unavoidable defeat of all that is great, but
He died to make us victors over sin, death, and despair.

For His cross was not the end (though there He surely came to a miserable end) but the great beginning; not defeat (though there He surely died a terrible death) but the grand victory, beside which every other victory is small and nothing and without which no one is able to win in the battle of life.

Now, who was the first to discover victory in the cross of Jesus? Whom did Christ permit to be the first to share in His victory?

There were the faithful, His disciples. They had hung on His every word and had given up everything for His sake. They had followed Him everywhere and had let Him send them into a hostile world. They had loyally shared His insecurity, had confessed and proclaimed Him, and in His name had done miracles. Were they the first?

There were those who loved Him; above all, His mother, who clung to Him as only a mother can cling to her son. She had borne Him after trustingly awaiting Him from God. She had reared Him and had observed His development with an anxious heart. Was she the first to share in the victory of Christ the King?

Or was it they whose diseases Christ had healed or whom He had even raised from the dead?

Or the scholars, who in devotion and meditation had given to the Scriptures a lifetime of devoted and searching study and held fast to those promises of God they were sure they must find and expect there — were they the first?

Or those conscientious people, devoted to duty, who took their calling seriously and hoped to please God by doing their duty in faithful obedience to their superiors? The soldiers and executioners, were they the ones?

No, it was not any of these! The one to whom the Lord gave the privilege of being the first to share in His victory was not faithful, not loving, not a scholar or a man bound to do his duty, but an outcast. He was a man who had grossly sinned against society and trampled on God's commandments. He was a robber who had attacked his own countrymen on the highway, had taken all they had, and perhaps even murdered them. A share in Christ's victory was given to one who could not claim any distinction. The victory was shared by one who had deserved nothing but execution.

None of the others experienced the victory of Jesus Christ. Most of the disciples had fled. His mother was frozen with hopeless anguish. The scholars by their ingenious theology had come to the honest conviction that Jesus could be nothing but a blasphemer. Zealous and conscientious men crucified Him in obedience to their orders.

The very virtues in which these all excelled were their downfall. The disciples fled because of their faithfulness, the mother was shocked into disbelief by her love, the theologians condemned Him because of their knowledge of Scripture, and the soldiers crucified Him because of their obedience and conscientiousness.

Had the disciples, after all their faithful allegiance, deserved this futility, this catastrophe — their Master on a cross? Had the mother deserved this anguish? Had the scribes, after all their diligent life's work, deserved to be made liars by Jesus' insignificance and His call to repentance? Had the dutiful men deserved to have their devotion to duty lead them astray and seduce them to sin?

They all answer no, no! And with this no they reject the cross of Jesus that would break them. Their excellencies come between them and the cross and bring about their fall. They insist that they are right in spite of the cross which God imposes and by which He proves them to be wrong in their expectations and claims. They insist on being right even against God. But in maintaining that they are right, they remain blind and deaf. The cross is for them nothing more than the egregious folly, the great failure, the plain insanity that it must be for every respectable person.

The only one crushed by the cross is the malefactor, who says: "And we indeed justly, for we receive the due reward of our deeds" (Luke 23:41). He is the only one of all people around Jesus on Calvary who once and for all has given up all claims that he is right. His only right is the right to reach the end and to die the death of a criminal. He has renounced every other right. The death penalty is all he has justly earned.

13

He is the only one who knows he is a sinner, and therefore he accepts the cross for himself and affirms it.

The attitude of all others under the cross — the anguish of His friends and the triumph of the enemies — implies reproach. His friends, for instance, in their hearts accuse Jesus because He did not use His miraculous power or at least did not avoid Jerusalem; His mother, because He did not preserve Himself for her; the scribes, because He was possessed by the devil; the decent people, because He violated order. They all blame Jesus. Only the malefactor who knows that he is guilty, so guilty that he stops making claims or uttering protests, only the man who breaks down completely under the burden of his sins and greets the cross as just reward — only he realizes that Jesus suffers innocently! Only he realizes that Jesus is condemned not for His own guilt but for a guilt which is not His own. Only he understands what it means that here on the cross is a man who before God is sinless. "We receive the due reward of our deeds; but this Man hath done nothing amiss" (verse 41).

By this declaration the malefactor becomes the first "evangelist" (as Augustine once said). Everyone else sees in Jesus only a man dying in utter helplessness. The malefactor alone, an obvious public enemy, realizes that sinlessness implies glory and a life without sin involves the most impressive display of energy and the greatest control of power. All others see merely that Jesus cannot move a muscle and can barely speak.

14

But the robber knows that a single word of this innocent Man can change everything, and he dares to ask something of Him who is so weak that He cannot even quench His thirst Himself. He alone sees the splendor of the victor's crown on Jesus' head and says, "Lord, remember me when Thou comest into Thy kingdom" (verse 42). Mighty Ruler, take me into Your kingdom. He alone recognizes in this crucified Man the Messiah, the Christ, the anointed King of God. The robber was the first of them all to share the victory of the cross. To him — and He does not let him wait — Jesus says, "Today shalt thou be with Me in Paradise." As Luther once said, the thug is "the real saint in the New Testament."

Can only a malefactor see Christ's victory on the cross and share this victory? Yes, only a malefactor! Let us once and for all lay aside the misleading moral ideas of everyday life. Let us face this fact: Before God there is no difference between lovelessness and murder, between hatred and homicide, between suspicion and highway robbery. Malefactors are we all, whether secretly or publicly, whether we are ready to admit it or not.

But the mere fact of being a malefactor does not guarantee an understanding of Christ's victory on the cross. Not solely as malefactors do we share the victory of the cross. There was a malefactor on the right hand and one on the left. Both approached Jesus in their last hour and both looked to Him for help. But only one of them was saved. The other cried, "Save Thyself and us." To be saved is not to be freed *from* the cross but *by* the cross! Christ is not touched by the cry, "Help us down from the cross, deliver us from the nails and the wood!" Christ hears him who is distressed because of the kind of life he has led and earnestly desires to have his sins expiated. The victory of the cross is given only to the malefactor who is crushed and asks not for the sparing of his life but asks for Jesus Himself. To die with Christ means for him life; to be ruled by Christ one day means to him salvation. We shall share the victory of Christ's cross not simply as malefactors but only as malefactors who collapse under the burden of their guilt and welcome the cross that God may be justified. Whoever refuses to be a malefactor will understand nothing, nothing at all of the cross of Christ. He will see only a drama with a tragic ending. He will see nothing of God's victory.

CHAPTER III

The Third Word on the Cross

Now there stood by the cross of Jesus His mother, and His mother's sister, Mary the wife of Cleophas, and Mary Magdalene. When Jesus therefore saw His mother, and the disciple standing by whom He loved, He saith unto His mother, Woman, behold thy son! Then saith He to the disciple, Behold thy mother! And from that hour that disciple took her unto his own home. (John 19:25-27)

CAN ANYONE really take the place of a son in the heart of a mother? Can a stranger suddenly be a son to her, that is, can she really feel that he is her son, can she really love him as her son? Could Mary forget that Son, could that Son be replaced, particularly that Son who came to such a fearful end on the cross?

Why didn't Jesus say, Mother, behold, I am entrusting you to John? Why didn't Jesus say to John, Take care of My mother? Why did He say, This is your son; this is your mother? He surely knew that a mother cannot really accept a stranger as her son even though he takes her to himself and cares for her as John undoubtedly did.

Why doesn't Jesus in this last hour say, Mother, I thank you? Why doesn't He console His mother? Why doesn't He at least call her "Mother"? Why this distant and impersonal address "Woman"? Doesn't Jesus want to be Mary's Son at least in death? How can this withdrawal from His mother be a sign of Jesus' love for her. Would it not have helped her more could she have been sure that the crucified Jesus considered Himself her Son and clung to her up to the last minute?

Such questions arise as we hear these words from the lips of the Crucified. But similar questions also arise in connection with certain words which Jesus had spoken earlier to His mother, when He traveled up and down the land, teaching and healing. When at Cana she asked Him to help the young bridal couple running short of wine, He turned to her and said, "Woman, what have I to do with thee?" (John 2:4). When later she came to Him with His brethren and He was told of her presence, He turned away and said, "Who is My mother or My brethren?" and turned to His disciples and said: "Whosoever shall do the will of God, the same is My brother and My sister and mother" (Mark 3:33, 35). The few Scripture passages which speak of the relationship of the adult Jesus to His mother again and again reveal on His part a peculiar reserve and aloofness. In another instance, when a woman in the company exclaimed, "Blessed is the womb that bare Thee, and the paps which Thou hast sucked," Jesus answered: "Yea, rather, blessed are they that hear the Word of God and keep it" (Luke 11:27 ff.). After all, Mary had awaited her Son in true faith in the promises of God, had borne Him in want and distress, and had lavished upon Him all the love with which a mother embraces her child and clings to him. But when He had grown up and gone forth after having been with John the Baptist, things turned out differently than she had expected.

Is it surprising that His mother felt insecure, that she did not understand Christ and became the image and prototype of all those "who are burdened with doubts about Jesus" (Bezzel)? In view of the radically different Messianic hopes which Mary probably shared with those of her day, should we consider it strange that at times she shared the opinion of many others that her Son was beside Himself (Mark 3:21)? What does the harsh aloofness and withdrawal of her Son mean? What is the meaning of His last word to His mother, who is no longer to be His mother?

It is hardly true, as some of the older interpreters suggest, that Jesus does not call His mother "mother" in order to spare her and not to increase her sorrow by using the name "mother." It hurts a mother more to be called "woman" by her child than to be called "mother." No, Jesus in His last hour actually withdraws from His mother as He had often done before. But the harshness of the Son is love. For the withdrawal of her Son is the approach and arrival of her God. This harshness and turning away robs Mary of her Son that she may recognize in Jesus the Son of God. The Jesus whom she bore is taken from her that she may see clearly the incarnate God and be adopted by Him. As yet she does not see the victory of the cross, she sees only the suffering of her child. She does not yet see God's kingdom coming with power into this world through the cross of Jesus; she sees only someone dying who belongs to her and whom she loves. Because of her mother love she cannot be confident like the malefactor, but must sorrow and lament; her love is actually blindness. Jesus wounds her mother love in this hour of decision in order to open her eyes to the God who can be found only on Calvary. He moves away from Mary that she may see her own salvation and the salvation of the whole world contained in the death of God's Son on the cross. Every pain inflicted on Mary points to the blessedness of that communion with God which can become hers only through the withdrawal of her Son. As Jesus, the Son of Man, separates Himself from His mother, the point at issue is her recognition of Jesus as the Son of God.

Could it have been different? Could this wound, this pain have been avoided? Must there be such harshness when God meets man? The pain was inevitable then and cannot be avoided now. So long as Mary still looked upon Jesus as the Son whom she had borne, so long as her thoughts, emotions, and sufferings centered here, she had not yet met God in Jesus. She had to forget that she had given birth to Jesus, and she must stop basing any claims on it. We may make claims on a son but not on God. We can look on a son, but never on God, as our own. God demands us as His own, and He makes one-sided claims. God is not in Jesus because Jesus is the Son of Mary. But God in His complete independence of men determined to become man through Mary, and He remains God. It is not the son of Mary who is the Son of God, but it is the Son of God who became the Son of Mary! He is much more than her Son. Jesus is the Savior in that He is the Word of God who became flesh.

Wounds and pain are unavoidable for Mary as well as for us when God reveals Himself. So long as we in any way imagine that we have a part in bringing about this revelation of God, as if we had helped to produce or cause His grace, we do not yet see God. So long as that which is distinctively God's activity is in any way dependent on what we do, we are not face to face with God's mercy and are not yet delivered from the wretched seesawing between our arrogance and despair.

God's love first appears by embracing us independently of our love or lack of love. We are safe in God only when we have not deserved God and when nothing therefore separates us from the love of God. Because this is and remains true, therefore God shatters everything that is idolatrous in those whom He loves. When a man makes his child his god, God will estrange the child from him — because God loves that man. When a nation puts nationalism in the place of God, God will crush this nationalism — because He wants to show love to that nation. When we think that we possess God because of our faithful attention to the duties of our calling or the steadfastness of our piety, God permits us to fail and to fall into depths where we can no more pray or be pious, but can only sob and sigh — because He loves us. Only him whom God does not love does He let alone with the gods of his own making and with a god whom he can control. We are not in God's hand until we meet the Son of God in His free grace (which is altogether independent of everything in this world) and all our claims on God are shattered. Because Jesus loves Mary, He shatters all her claims on Him and puts her into the position of the malefactor who has no more claims to present and therefore is made happy in God.

And what then? Then a life begins in which we no longer own anything but receive everything, in which we no longer make claims but gladly accept His gifts, in which we no longer brood but believe. Then a life begins in which we experience that God gives us much more than we could give or even take for ourselves. And with it begins the communion of believers in which and through which God works in free grace. By binding His mother to the disciple and the disciple to His mother, the crucified Christ directs her into the communion of believers in which we find a grateful Mary after Easter. This communion is not determined by flesh and blood but by the Word of Jesus. But this communion is so intimate and rich in fulfillment that Jesus describes it by using the terms "mother" and "son." Indeed, Jesus blesses Mary by a withdrawing from her. For the communion of believers is greater than any natural communion. It is communion with God.

CHAPTER IV

The Fourth Word on the Cross

After this, Jesus, knowing that all things were now accomplished that the Scripture might be fulfilled, saith, I thirst. (John 19:28)

IS IT NOT a monstrous blasphemy of divine majesty even to speak about God on the cross? God, the Almighty and Holy, cannot possibly be found on the cross, the place of failure and disgrace! Doesn't the word of the cross at once deny God's majesty and destroy man's dignity? Humanity cannot possibly recognize as its Captain one who is executed without resistance, and cannot find its perfection in this image of misery and grief. What happens to the glory and grandeur of our destiny which is striving for realization within us?

As we see the Crucified thirsting and accepting refreshment from His executioners, doesn't this thirst give the lie to what has been said about the Son of divine majesty, not to speak of that Son's God-forsakenness and His death? At the wedding of Cana He had changed water into wine in His all-surpassing power (John 2:1-11); at Jacob's well He had offered the woman of Samaria water which would relieve her thirst forever (John 4:1-29); He had promised that rivers of living water should flow out from all who believe in Him (John 7:38). And now in His thirst this same Jesus is to be helplessly dependent on His enemies? Doesn't the almighty, holy God here deny Himself?

So long as we still imagine that we must praise God's majesty and protect it against lowliness, we have not yet passionately sought God. So long as we still rave about His omnipotence and holiness in contrast to the weakness and disgrace of the cross, we have not yet been confronted by God's majesty and have not yet learned to know ourselves.

Face the reality of our world with its rise and fall, with its heights and depths, with its revolts and suppressions, with its paradox of abundance and want, with its chorus of victors and victims, healthy people, sick people, dying people, with all its thirst for life and yearning for peace! In the face of this let us take seriously the statement concerning God's unlimited omnipotence, and then realize that this chaos with its shameful injustice and destruction would be impossible if Almighty God, whom no one can resist, did not permit it to continue. Let us take seriously the fact that God is the Lord, and not try to make of Him a mere thing alongside all the other things of this world. Then we shall be paralyzed with terror before Almighty God, who is able to change everything but who seems to will all this confusion and horror.

Look for God on the way in which He wishes to help us. Walk the way of obedience that God has shown us by His commandments. Take seriously His promise that He will be a Savior and Help for those who obey. Examine your own obedience day by day, your own life with its intentions and accomplishments, with its thoughts and works, with its struggle for the obedience of love toward God and man, and with all its defeats. And then we shall tremble and quake before the Holy God whom we cannot satisfy and before whom everything remains corrupt and vain. We shall be filled with fear as in trying to obey God we only realize the magnitude of the divine demand, and as in our every attempt to obey we become only more disobedient. Then we thirst for God — but the Holy One is beyond the sinner's reach.

God's majesty is not to be praised. It drives us to despair and terrifying misery. God's omnipotence crushes us in its aloofness from our distress, God's holiness damns us by its complete withdrawal from us sinners. We should be silent about God rather than mention His name, should forget Him rather than search for Him if we were not compelled to search for Him again and again. Without Christ, the majesty of God means only gruesome distance and terrible anger. We want to flee from it, but don't know where.

We wish that we were no longer human beings — perhaps a bush, a stone, or anything else — only not a human being who thinks and must go on thinking, who suffers under sin and yet cannot escape it, who yearns for God, but is crushed by God's remoteness and unapproachableness. There is no such thing as human dignity in the face of God's majesty.

Now look up to the Sufferer on the cross and listen: Here is God! Look at Him in His thirst and know this: Our thirst torments Him! His thirst actually is the terrible thirst of a dying man, whose mouth is convulsed in the struggle of death. And so no other thirst is strange to Him. See this torture in its highest degree! If God's Son endures it, then God is no longer far away, then the Almighty and Holy One shares our suffering and assumes it completely.

Continue to look and see how they give Him something to drink! His thirst seems to be unquenchable. Again and again it is quenched, quenched of all things through the sponge offered by the very men who have beaten and crucified Him. The Son of divine majesty, the Christ of supernatural fullness of power, has become so lowly that He lets men give Him drink, so weak and helpless that nothing seems so fitting as ridicule and derision. Behold this disgrace! God's terrifying greatness has vanished in the crucified One. God is here in the midst of us — the Most Lowly and the Most Humble.

Nothing is greater in this scene than that here

27

God ceases to insist on His greatness and descends to become the lowliest among us. Nothing is holier than this, that God surrenders His unapproachable holiness and, made to be sin, gives holiness to us sinners. Nothing is truly more divine than that God — to speak foolishly — finally contradicts Himself and offends His own majesty. Were it not for this, we must all perish. We cannot live under the wrath of the overwhelming God. Whoever thinks he can, has not yet been confronted by God's greatness. We can only deny God or curse ourselves. But we cannot establish communion with God.

Therefore it is not enough merely to *see* Jesus on the cross. It is of no help to us merely to *see* how the sponge is offered to Jesus and moistens His lips. But is it not possible that when we thus speak of His thirst and agony and tormenting pain we voice only our own interpretation? If everything depends on the fact that God has really become man, then it is most important that Jesus Himself *speaks* of His thirst and that He cries out, "I thirst." Our eyes cannot observe with certainty that the Son of God really suffered. We could doubt and think that God's Son did not really feel the suffering, that His soul was spared all torments. We might say His physical hanging on the cross is an act of make-believe; in reality He is majestically far removed from all suffering. But this doubt is utterly denied by His anguished cry. The cry of the

Son of God expresses real suffering and pain. By this cry we are assured that He has truly and really suffered and felt all of the agonies of the cross with all their physical pain. God has really become one of us.

CHAPTER V

The Fifth Word on the Cross

And about the ninth hour Jesus cried with a loud voice, saying, Eli, Eli, lama sabachthani? That is to say, My God, My God, why hast Thou forsaken Me? (Matt. 27:46)

BEHOLD THE MAN on the cross! His body is contorted in agony, His ashen face is streaked with blood, His features reveal His extremity! Behold the Man, His body broken, suspended on the cross as a criminal! This is not a sinner such as we are; He is the Christ, the Son of God. Look at the cross: God is there! Only there can God be found!

What is the meaning of the fearful cry, "My God, My God, why hast Thou forsaken Me?" It is dreadful enough and hard to understand that the Christ of God, the Son of God, endured reviling, smiting, and the cross. But this cry is the quintessence of everything dreadful, far exceeding in frightfulness even the suffering of the cross: God's Son forsaken by God! His thirst was much more than a physical thirst, it was a thirst for

30

God. The Christ of God is cast into godlessness in the original and truest sense of this word. Can this be so? Is there no way of escape from this cry?

As we examine the history of interpretation of this word in Christendom during the past two thousand years, we meet repeated attempts to escape from the stark horror of this word and to flee from it. Some say: Jesus spoke this word for us; for He was never forsaken by God, but we were (Theophylact). Others say: Jesus does not pray for Himself, but in place of the Jews, whom God has forsaken since they have crucified Jesus. Or, the forsakenness applies only to Jesus' body (Thomas Aquinas). Again others say: When Jesus said, "My God, My God, why hast Thou forsaken Me?" He did not think primarily of the beginning of Psalm 22, but of the whole psalm, and in this psalm we also read: "The meek shall eat and be satisfied; they shall praise the Lord that see Him" (verse 26). And finally Schleiermacher: "We may safely conclude from the application which the Savior made of this holy hymn to Himself . . . that also in this moment . . . He thought and felt about His death as clearly and calmly as we find Him doing everywhere in those last addresses by which He sought to prepare His disciples for His death."

But all interpretations of this nature are nothing but attempts to flee from the cross of Christ. If God had not forsaken Jesus, He would not have uttered the plaint that He did. If Jesus had not been without

God, He would not have "cried" this very psalm verse "with a loud voice." And when He cried, "My God, My God," He indeed still called Him *"My* God," the God who until now had always been His and had proved Himself to be His God in a thousand ways. But as He was dying on Calvary, this God, His God had vanished. Jesus called God "My God" because of the past, because of His yearning, and because the words of Scripture in which He found His forsakenness portrayed permitted Him to use them. The Crucified One cried out in the words of Scripture in which He had lived His life, but He cried out as one truly separated from God. As Luther says, "Christ was damned and abandoned more than all the saints." If we evade this fact, we turn away from the comfort of the cross and of grace altogether.

What is the meaning of: Jesus was forsaken by God? He who had said of Himself: "I and My Father are one" (John 10:30), and: "He that hath seen Me hath seen the Father" (John 14:9) — this Jesus no longer saw the Father, this Jesus was without God. Instead of divine strength, there was within Him only a wretched barrenness. In place of divine intimacy only an impenetrable, terrible wall. His prayers received no answer, His weeping no comfort. God had no relief for His Son. Turning away from Him, God turned all the more on Him with His terrible wrath. God made the Christ god-less and subjected Him to His terrible judgment. God deprived the innocent

Christ of His own most proper right and cast Him away into guilt and perdition. We human beings have ridiculed and forsaken Christ. But God Himself was the cause of His most terrible abandonment. We have tortured and crucified Him. But God Himself inflicted upon Him the greatest torment. Even if men had wanted to, they could not have disturbed the communion between God and the Son of God. God Himself withdrew from Him. And precisely thereby God intervened in the happening on Calvary and made it the decisive event of all time.

Only by forsaking His Son does God make Him like unto us in every respect. True, He was like us in His flesh and blood; He was like us also in His pains. But there is an agony far more terrible than these. Only through His unfathomable Godforsakenness does Christ completely take our place: He suffers all that really was ours. He suffers the separation from God that hung over all us sinners. He beats against the wall against which, inexorable to our yearning, all of us would dash ourselves to death if it were not for Him. The very wrath under which we stand, the very judgment pronounced upon our sins, strike Him. Our punishment is laid on the Innocent One. When God forsook Jesus Christ, He "made Him to be sin for us who knew no sin" (2 Cor. 5:21). Thus God makes Him entirely like us.

Christ's loud lamenting His being forsaken by God therefore involves this message: Men, hear this: God again turns to you — God punishes Me; God takes away your punishment — God crushes Me beneath His anger. God lifts you up in His love. By sentencing His Son, God terminates His condemnation of us. By rejecting Christ He again receives us as His own. For God rejects only sin and judges only guilt. He rejects no one who is innocent. He condemns no son who has remained faithful to Him. He rejects Christ in our stead and condemns His Son in order to forgive us. God forsakes the Crucified One means: He accepts the sacrifice of His Son.

Everything depends on this, that the Crucified One was really forsaken by God. Therefore this desperate cry: "My God, My God, why hast Thou forsaken Me?" is the most comforting of the seven words of our Lord on the cross. Indeed, it is perhaps the most comforting word of the entire Bible. In any case, there is no comfort either in the Old or in the New Testament that does not have its ultimate foundation in this cry of agony.

Therefore this is true: Since Christ was forsaken by God, there is no longer any abandonment by God. If you think you are forsaken by God, then look at Christ! If you believe in Christ, Christ was forsaken by God in your stead, and in His stead you have communion with God. Since Christ suffered the wrath of God, there is no longer a despair that is irremovable. If your guilt oppresses you and you fear your sin is so great that God cannot forgive it, you are in error.

Since you are a Christian, you know that the Son of God was made to be sin in your stead and was punished for you, but you, O sinner, are without sin!

The cry, "I thirst," showed that Christ suffers in His physical nature as we do. This cry of being forsaken by God proclaims that God's Son is without God like us. The other word revealed not only that Christ was mistreated in His body, but also that He was conscious of every mistreatment. This word says: Christ was forsaken not only by the pious and righteous among His people but also by His heavenly Father. Both words together say: Christ suffered both in His body and in His spirit. He was spared nothing at all by God and by man. He bore all our distress, and there is none that He did not bear.

Thank Christ for His suffering by believing and holding fast to the truth that all your troubles can no longer be the final and ultimate suffering! Before you ever lived, He took it from you and bore it. Your sin is forgiven, and your loneliness is ended.

CHAPTER VI

The Sixth Word on the Cross

And when Jesus had cried with a loud voice He said, Father, into Thy hands I commend My spirit. (Luke 23:46)

AND NOW marvel at the next word uttered by Jesus in His thirst and Godforsakenness. Hear the cry of the dying Savior, wonder and continue to marvel until you are healed once for all.

The dying Man on the cross cries, "Father." He speaks of One who watches over Him and provides for Him with a father's love. He speaks of One who belongs to Him and is merciful as fathers are merciful. He addresses God the Almighty and Holy One, the Lord over all that happens, over joy and sorrow, life and death as Father.

But He feels nothing of God's love and fatherly affection, nothing of His care and mercy. He feels only the terror of being forsaken by God and experiences nothing but the terrible judgment of God.

He calls the angry God "Father," and thus He calls destruction providence, and forsakenness mercy.

He continues: "I commend." Commending is more than asking and hoping; commending means entrusting, delivering. He not only desires something from God, but at once regards His desire as fulfilled. His cry is not a prayer like our uncertain calling and hoping, but a prayer anticipating fulfillment with full assurance. He accomplishes that for which He asks. Jesus prays: God, accept My soul, and at the same time He delivers it to Him. This prayer is not the asking of questions or a mere attempt, but the surest communion and consent.

But there is no communication whatever between Him and God. He feels only that God has broken all relations with Him. He feels only that He has nothing in common with God. He is fully experiencing the fact that one cannot commend anything to the angry God, but can only suffer under Him.

And as Jesus commends His spirit into God's "hands," He speaks of hands opening above Him to bless Him. He speaks of God extending His hands in fatherly goodness to take Him and draw Him to His heart.

But He feels only that God has completely turned away. God is far away. He has withdrawn His hand from His Son, and this Son stands there under God's judgment.

Let no one cease marveling and wondering as Jesus,

forsaken by God, calls, "Father, into Thy hands I commend My spirit." In all of His experiences on the cross, external and internal, physical and spiritual, in all that He sees and suffers, there is nothing to encourage Him to utter such a plea. Forsaken by God He can have no reason for trusting in the angry God as a helpful Father. The only relief He feels is the vinegar that the soldiers offer Him. Just because the God-forsaken Jesus has no good reason for trusting in God this trusting word is closely connected with the complaint of being forsaken by God (even though the order of the words on the cross was perhaps a different one). When Jesus quotes a word from the Psalms: "Father, into Thy hands I commend My spirit," He acts contrary to all experience and all reason. He does something which is altogether unsupported and unreasonable. The meaning, then, of Jesus' entrusting words is that Jesus believes.

Let us try to make clear to ourselves what this means. Let us attempt to follow Him in believing, since He has shown us the way. What would His believing cry mean if we were to utter it? When God is far away, He is close to us. When God's judgment casts us down, God is gracious. When our prayers rebound to us, God hears us. When our sin seems endless, we are holy. Collapse is no longer collapse, but building; failure is no longer failure, but progress; destruction is no longer destruction, but consummation. When everything crashes down upon us and nothing is left, then God's nearness is greatest. When we can see no way out, then God has already prepared His way for us. "To proclaim and believe the Gospel of the cross means this: Cross is glory; death, life; sin, righteousness; curse, blessing; our lost condition, salvation." "When God thus makes alive, He does it by slaying; when He justifies, He does it by making guilty; when He leads us into heaven, He does it by leading us to hell." "Really every extreme becomes the extreme of all . . . : great temptation is no temptation; utmost confusion is serenest peace; greatest sin, greatest righteousness; greatest folly, greatest wisdom." (Luther)

If we believed as Jesus believed, we would be firm as granite. Then nothing could hurt us any longer, nothing could sadden us, nothing could separate us from God's love in all eternity; then we would be inseparably united with God. We would no longer depend on special experiences of God's presence, which again yield to experiences of God's distance. God would always be present, not only now and then. God would be there entirely, not weaker at one time and stronger at another. If we believed in this manner, we could outrun the reality of our senses. There would be no more unpleasant experiences. God Himself would be with us.

But wouldn't it be madly presumptuous on our part to dare what the Son of God dared? Wouldn't this be a piece of outrageous familiarity and disrespect for divine sovereignty, which is surely not proper for us? Would it not be the height of sin to leap to God in this manner and to conquer Him? Indeed, we sinners wouldn't reach God even if we leaped. God would not catch us. We would surely be wrecked and be hurled into the deepest abyss to our destruction. If we by ourselves were to attempt what Jesus did, we would only reach the height of sin, but not God. And though we called "Father" a thousand times, and again and again commended ourselves to Him, He would not receive us into His hands.

There was only One who could call the distant God "Father," and that One was Jesus Christ. Only One could ask of God and be heard — Jesus, God's Son. There is no faith except the faith of Jesus Christ. No faith leads to God unless it is the faith of this crucified Lord. Faith saves us only if it is at the same time the faith of Jesus Christ. There is no victory of faith except in faith in the Son of God. We must believe in Him who alone could leap to God because He had never committed a sin. Only in the faith of the God-forsaken Son of God is the visible world overcome. Only in the faith in the God-forsaken Son of God do we become victors. Only by His innocent death has the wall between God and the sinner been removed.

But if we believe in Christ, then that which we can see and experience has been judged by God, and the whole God is there for us. Then no boldness of faith is too great, and no contempt of unpleasant experiences too daring. Then being forsaken by God is no longer God-forsakenness, but God-nearness; then our sin is no longer sin, but righteousness; trouble is blessing; then war is peace, and death is life. Then also the converse is true: "No danger is the greatest of all dangers, and the greatest security is the mightiest temptation" (Luther). If we believe in Christ, then God is our Father extending His hands to us. Then our prayers are heard, and we cannot pray too trustingly and confidently. Then we can receive even while we pray, and thank God for receiving what we ask for even while we are still asking, although we have not yet received it. In obedience to the Cross of Christ no prayer is too bold. For when Christ cried out: "Father, into Thy hands I commend My spirit," He "collected our souls in a bundle" and delivered them to God with His own (Calvin).

CHAPTER VII

The Seventh Word on the Cross

When Jesus therefore had received the vinegar, He said, It is finished; and He bowed His head and gave up the ghost. (John 19:30)

WHAT IS FINISHED? He who promised rivers of living water in His dying moments cries, "I thirst." He who said of Himself, "I and My Father are one," is forsaken by God on the cross. He who invited all who are weary to come to Him to give them life is the most miserable of all the miserable. He remains helpless and dies.

What is finished? The innocent Man on the cross dies the death of a criminal, the guilty stand scot-free under the cross and continue to live, and are even to receive forgiveness. The faithful followers prove themselves unfaithful under the cross, and the outlaw, the malefactor, the enemy of the divine commandments, suddenly proves to be God's friend. The mother is harshly deprived of the Son given by God, but by this very act the Son of divine love is to be given to her.

Isn't all this the height of nonsense? Isn't all this a hodgepodge of contradictions of which only one should be sufficient to demonstrate the foolishness of the whole affair? Isn't the cross obviously a magnificent failure? Shouldn't we speak of destruction rather than "finishing," of the end and the collapse rather than of the completion?

Yes, the cross is failure, collapse, and destruction. The cross is absurdity and foolishness. Thank God that this is so! Only because the cross is an absurdity, the misery of our human wisdom finally is ended. Only because it is a failure, the failure of our life, unhappy despite all success, is finally removed. For since an innocent Man is the heart and center of the absurdities of Calvary, the cross is the greatest wisdom. Because God Himself submitted to the failure of the cross, therefore the cross is everlasting completion.

What is finished? "All was now finished" (John 19:28, RSV): not only Jesus' suffering and commission but also we; not only we but the whole world. Nothing remains to be supplied or to be added by man for the salvation of the world.

When the community of Jesus Christ confesses: All was now finished on the cross, the little word "all" dare not be understood as an expression of an exaggerated enthusiasm not to be taken literally. This word cannot be understood concretely and yet comprehensively and all-inclusively enough. Our sin, too, is inconceivably great, and we cannot ever picture its devastating results as concretely and as extensively as they are. The human will is corrupt. We not only commit sins, but we are sinners through and through. We have lost the freedom to obey, and by ourselves cannot find the way back to God. Decision and action, consideration and decision, are fettered by the curse of being servants and slaves of enmity against God. Human nature is corrupt. Not only are we sinners in thought and deed, but also our entire life is defiled in soul and body. There is no death in God; His creative will is life. Death is the curse of sin. Our separation from God cast us away into the up and down of becoming and passing away, of life and death. To adore this rhythm is to romanticize. With man there fell into the dominion of death and impermanence the whole creation, "made subject to vanity, not willingly," waiting with "earnest expectation," "groaning and travailing in pain" with us (Rom. 8:19 ff.). The result of sin is a world corrupt. Creation lies desolate. What we now see is divine creation, human devastation, and divine judgment in confusion. The world no longer presents the creative ordinances of the beginning and shows us no way back to God, the Creator and Lord.

As God was dishonored by us, so He was honored and praised by Jesus' death. As a world was ruined by sin, so a world was created and finished on the cross.

44

Yes, indeed, the results of Jesus' death on the cross extend infinitely far. The complete corruption of body and soul, of man and creation, has now been healed. The separation between God and man is now removed. God is again manifest and near. Sin no longer separates us from God. The power of sin has ended. Gone is the inability of the will to accomplish its ends. Our will is obedient, and obedience is now service to God. We are now the children of God, we are new. Death no longer rules, we live the life eternal. Gone now are curse and exile! The enslavement of the whole world is past. Man and creation are free. A new world is here without death and without guilt. Fallen creation has been redeemed, a new creation is finished.

But isn't everything altogether different in reality? Our life still reaches a limit, and death still rules as before. Existence still consumes itself — in ups and downs, and no kingdom of the world abides forever. Within us and about us everything remains as before — rising and declining, running, falling and rising, and again falling and rising. Where is the victory over sin? It still assails us as before, and again and again we are defeated. Where is the new man in his purity? Where is his new immortal body? Where is the victory of Jesus Christ?

Isn't this perhaps the most we can say: We hope that sometime in the future things will be different and that God will someday complete His new world? Must we not be content to say: Forgiveness was accomplished on the cross, but everything else is still to come and can only be wished and hoped for — if after almost two thousand years of waiting we may still dare to hope? How can He say: All is accomplished?

Paul knows all of these objections when he says, "We *are* justified," that is, acquitted, in the future judgment of the world. He even says, "We are risen" (Col. 3:1); that is, at the future resurrection of the dead. He knows very well that the flesh still wars against the spirit and that creation waits for the manifestation of the sons of God. But still he says: "Old things are passed away; behold, all things are become new" (2 Cor. 5:17). All contradictions these, and yet most positive reality. In Christ he is justified, he is risen! In Christ time has been overcome; a new world has replaced the old.

All is accomplished on the cross, because Jesus finished the work assigned to Him by God and because Jesus united us, His own, with Himself forever. By taking our place on the cross Jesus put us in His place. By no longer seeing God in His forsakenness He tore open the heavens for us that we might see and honor the Father. Our sin became His sin that His righteousness might become ours. Our death became His death that His life might become ours. What was ours became His, so that what is His might become ours. But if the union is so close, then also His future is our future. Then nothing can separate us from Him when He rises on the third day. His resurrection is also our resurrection. His new body is our body. Then nothing can separate us from Him when He ascends to the Father in heaven. Then we are just as much His own when He returns to judge the world. The sentence of condemnation does not strike us. God's Son shared our transitoriness, and now His own for all eternity share His imperishable glory.

All this lies in the future, and yet it is finished and is in the present. For God's future is a greater reality than is the human present. God's promise is a fact more concrete than is human history. What God says is more real than what we do. With God decision and action are not two separate actions as with us, but both are one. God's future is more sure than the human present, and the sequence of this world is changed by God's revelation. If we believe, then God's future is the present, and the human present becomes the past. If we believe in the crucified Savior, if we are crushed by His cross, and if, like the malefactor, we look only to Jesus, then we see the Father whose kingdom is among us.

We are engaged in the battle of this world, and woe unto us before God if we do not take this battle seriously! But if we believe in Jesus Christ, this battle is already decided even though man's history ·in its larger and smaller aspects is growing more savage and anti-God. We are fighting a battle within us between sin and God's call, and woe unto us if we do not fight this decisive battle to the bitter end!

47

But if we believe in Christ, the victory has already been won. We must wait for the return of the Lord at the end of time. Woe unto us if we no longer want to wait! But in faith we also know that the Lord is among us and that He rules. Again and again we dishonor God, and we still suffer under the wrath of God. But in Christ our sin is righteousness, and God's wrath is love. All this is reality. For our present became His that His future might be ours. The visible world and time were judged once for all on the cross.

The new world is finished, no matter how much our world is writhing in convulsions. The kingdom of God is accomplished, even though the churches and kingdoms of this world struggle so hard against it. To all of us who think that we are in a stage of transition or even only in the beginning, who are vexed by the little that we accomplish and the great things that we resolve with a holy intention and do not accomplish — also to us sinners it is said: It is finished! Jesus' work is accomplished, God is glorified on the earth. In fact, so completely is it finished on the cross that nothing, nothing at all, could be added by man.

CHAPTER VIII

Prayer

Lord God, Father in heaven,
Lord God, Son, Savior of the world,
Lord God, Holy Ghost,
Have mercy upon us!

Lord God, Father in heaven,
Who didst not spare Thine own Son,
But didst deliver Him up for us all,
Him, who knew no sin
Thou didst make to be sin for us
And hast committed unto us the Word of
    reconciliation,
Be merciful to us, help us, Lord and God!

Jesus Christ, God's Son,
Who for the joy that was set before Thee
Didst endure the cross,
Despising the shame,
Didst become poor for our sakes,
In all points tempted like as we are,

Delivered into the hands of sinners,
Didst taste the bitterness of death
And the deepest distress of God-forsakenness,
Didst learn obedience by the things which Thou
    didst suffer,
Didst become obedient unto death, even the death
    of the cross,
Thou Lamb of God, that didst take away the sin
    of the world,
Have mercy upon us!

We poor sinners implore Thee, O holy and faithful
    Jesus
That by the power of Thy suffering
Thou wouldst save us from all sin,
From hatred and envy,
From pride and loveless judging,
From selfishness and hardheartedness,
From indolence and unwillingness to bear
    the cross,
From coldness and desire to please men,
Thou wouldst save us, O holy Jesus,
And give us power to become the sons of God,
That we may follow Thee as true disciples
In meekness and humility;
Take our cross upon us,
Cry to the Father when we are forsaken,
Commit our spirit into His hands,
In the battle against sin,

In the hour of temptation,
In the darkness of assault,
Against depressing thoughts,
In the final hour of need,
Help us, Lord Jesus Christ!

Gather under Thy cross the children of God
    scattered in the world.
Bring hither those still far away,
Recall the lost,
Bring home the erring,
Go out to the seeking,
Help us to become one that we love one another
And from our heart forgive one another.
Thou, our Peace,
Grant us Thy peace!

Jesus Christ, God's Son,
O Thou Lamb of God, that takest away the sin
    of the world,
        have mercy upon us!
O Thou Lamb of God, that takest away the sin
    of the world,
        have mercy upon us!
O Thou Lamb of God, that takest away the sin
    of the world,
        grant us Thy peace!
Lord, have mercy,
Christ, have mercy,
Lord, have mercy upon us!

CHAPTER IX

The First Word of the Risen Lord

Mary said unto them: Because they have taken away my Lord, and I know not where they have laid Him. And when she had thus said, she turned herself back and saw Jesus standing and knew not that it was Jesus. Jesus saith unto her, Woman, why weepest thou? Whom seekest thou? She, supposing Him to be the gardener, saith unto Him, Sir, if Thou have borne Him hence, tell me where thou hast laid Him, and I will take Him away. Jesus saith unto her, Mary. She turned herself and saith unto Him, Rabboni, which is to say, Master. Jesus saith unto her, Touch Me not; for I am not yet ascended to My Father, but go to My brethren, and say unto them, I ascend unto My Father and your Father, and to My God and your God. (John 20:13-17)

MARY MAGDALENE has every reason to rejoice aloud, but she weeps. She has already been found by Jesus, but she believes that she is still a seeker who does not find Him. Indeed, while she already sees Him, she is still one who does not see Him. And while Jesus is already speaking to her she still thinks that she is forgotten and nameless — a poor, lost woman.

52

All of the Easter stories begin with tears, blindness, and fear. The disciples as well as the women are terrified at the empty grave, at the angels, at the risen Lord who appears to them. The Christ who entered Jerusalem for His Passion they greeted with joy and shouting. The Christ who is risen from the dead they meet with despair and fear. At the beginning of the Passion story there is joy and shouting, although it was evident from Christ's words that He would suffer and die. At the beginning of the Easter story there is sorrow and hopelessness, although one could know from Jesus' words that He would rise on the third day. We are so blind! Our heart is so full of contradictions that we rejoice where we should be afraid, and we are terrified where there is reason for great joy. But all presumptuousness and all fear, all sadness and all false joy are wiped out by the resurrection of Jesus Christ.

God has raised the crucified Jesus from the dead. Thereby He approves this death and loudly proclaims: He did not die, as did all others, because of His own sin. Even though I, God, made Him to be sin, He did not die as a sinner. Even though I Myself condemned Him to death, this verdict was not the judgment of His life. He was made sin and condemned for the sin of others. He died innocently, even though you men after His death opened His body with a spear, rolled a great stone before His grave, and set a guard over the grave in order to be absolutely sure of His death as a criminal.

Not only was the crucified Savior raised from the

dead; He Himself also arose in the grave. Not only did He as a corpse receive life but He the corpse also laid hold on life: "I have power to lay it down, and I have power to take it again" (John 10:18). In his glorious self-resurrection Jesus proves Himself to be what He had not ceased to be even in His deepest humiliation, the Son of God. When on the third day the crucified Lord Himself removes the stone rolled before His grave, steps over the soldiers stationed there as a guard, and breaks through the grief by which His friends tried to hold Him in the grave, He thereby reveals that it was really God who suffered on the cross. The Lord of Life became a slave of death for us; the Holy One made Himself to be sin and dust for us — and this Lord of all lords took up His life again in the grave. Neither in the incarnation nor on the cross nor after the cross in the realm of the dead did God's Son ever cease to be God's Son. Hear it, all mankind, God Himself bore all of your misery!

The risen Lord reveals Himself to this tortured and weeping woman as He called her by her name, "Mary." With this call He firmly embraces her as His very own: "I have called thee by thy name; thou art Mine" (Is. 43:1). Calling her by her name "Mary" therefore implies: Do not cry, do not fear, do not search any more; you are found, you are Mine for time and eternity!

Mary did not yet believe in the resurrection of

the Crucified One even in the face of the empty grave and the angels and their words. Not even when she saw the risen Lord did she believe — until He spoke to her. Even when He addressed her with "Woman," or when He asked, "Why weepest thou?" she did not recognize the risen Lord but only when He called her "Mary" and thereby promised her, "Thou art Mine." The designation "Woman" might have been intended for any other woman. By addressing her personally He concentrates on speaking to her especially. Thereby He breaks through the blind interest which all, friend and foe, showed in His corpse, even though it were only to honor Him by their grief.

Mary's blindness is for us the gracious invitation to believe. For we need not be afraid and think it was easier for her than for us to believe the risen Lord because she saw Him. She did not believe because she saw Him, but because He called her. And He also knows and calls each one of us. The fact that Mary did not recognize the risen Lord even on the evidence of the empty tomb and of the angels, and that she did not recognize Him even when He appeared is an invitation to us. We have seen neither the risen Lord nor the empty grave nor the angels in the grave, and yet we are not at a disadvantage over against this woman. For her as well as for us blindness is pierced only when He speaks to us. No one has an advantage or a disadvantage. The risen Lord meets everyone in His Word.

The moment of the resurrection itself, however, remains God's very own eternal secret. No human eye was permitted to watch as the dead body of Jesus became alive in the grave and the crucified Lord left the grave.

With the call "Mary" the risen Lord caught up this woman into His sweep from the grave to the ascension into heaven. His call implies: You are Mine, come along! Hasten with Me to the royal dominion which I assume at the right hand of God. Forget your own ways of hope and despondency, of enthusiasm and fear. To be called by name by the risen Christ means that we now have a Lord who makes us lords.

Mary Magdalene is blind not only before she recognizes the Lord but also when she recognizes Him. She is blind in that she fails not only to recognize Him but also to acknowledge Him as the risen Lord. She embraces Him in order to hold Him. She grasps Him as she had probably grasped Him before, and she wants the past to be once more the present. She clings to Jesus' former lowliness, whereas it is His glory that confronts her as He hastens on His way to complete glorification. This attitude is expressed perhaps also by her answer, "Rabboni." When she mistook the Lord for the gardener, she called Him "Sir"; but when she recognized Him, she called Him "Rabbi," Teacher, Master, just as the disciples had called Him in His days on earth. "Mary Magdalene thinks that He has risen to live with them again as

He had heretofore, as she had seen Lazarus and others whom Christ had raised from the dead associate with people as they had done before. She didn't recall that He was to begin a different and eternal life" (Luther). To the last she struggles against the risen Lord and His victory.

"Over against this Christ says: No, My dear Mary, I'll not let you touch Me in this manner. I did not rise from the dead for such a purpose. I am now in a different state and life. I am King and Lord over all that exists" (Luther). "Touch Me not," let Me go, don't hold Me, don't detain Me. "For I am not yet ascended to My Father," I am in a hurry, hurrying to occupy the throne in heaven prepared for Me at the right hand of God, My Father. "This is the meaning of these words: The state of the resurrection is not yet complete and final in all points until the risen Lord sits in heaven at the right hand of God. Therefore the women do wrong because, satisfied with half of the resurrection, they desire merely His presence in this world" (Calvin). But His leaving this world becomes a greater presence, and the end of the visible, earthly communion becomes an incomparably more intimate eternal communion. Then the risen Lord is no longer only here or there, but at all times He is everywhere among all who call upon Him.

As one in a hurry, the risen Lord gives the command to hurry: "Go to My brethren and say to them." He hurries away from them not only at His ascension into heaven but in all of His appearances, beginning with Easter. As soon as He has established faith and has given His commission He disappears, and so by His very disappearance He counsels: You have here no continuing city. Hurry, hurry!

"I ascend unto My Father and your Father and to My God and your God." Not until after His resurrection, according to the witness of St. John, does Jesus say, "My Father" is "your Father." He first had to die for His disciples and proclaim His substitutionary death by His resurrection. His Father is their Father because the beloved Son first became for them, His enemies, an enemy whom God slew. In the crucified Lord who rose again they are now sons. "My God" is "your God" also says this: As God did not leave Jesus in the grave, so He will not leave you in the grave either. As God exalts Jesus, so He will also exalt you that you with Him shall judge the world. Nothing can any longer separate you from Him.

And now, men and women, hasten to proclaim this to all. If you hear of the risen Lord but remain silent, you will not be sure of Him. If you recognize the risen Lord only as being in the past, you have not known Him. If you think of the risen Lord but remain at your place, He will not be your own. Sure of the risen Lord is only he who is hurrying toward His return, the revelation of His glory. He is the Victory only for him who stands before all men and confesses Christ's victory before all the world and never ceases to cry aloud: He is the Son, the Son alone is the Victor, in Him alone God is your God and your Father.

But aren't Christ and His people separated like the words "mine" and "thine"? After all, He does not say, "our Father," but "My Father" and "your Father." He doesn't say, "our God," but "My God" and "your God."

This distinction is not a wall of separation. It is the closest union. It does not break but most strongly confirms our communion with Him. Whoever overlooks this distinction will lose his communion with the Father and the Son. Whoever respects this distinction will be a joint heir with Christ and God's son forever. For everything is established in Him, the one, eternal Son, who died for us. He led the way, not we. He made us God's children, but He did not need us to be God's Son. Only as we honor Christ as different from us do we become like Him. Only as we distinguish between Him and us, all distinctions pass away. "Believe the Word only, boast of and insist on this truth that Christ wants to be your Brother. Then God will be your Father; then all the angels will be your friends; then sun, moon, and stars must laugh and rejoice with you; hell must be shut down completely; and there must be nothing left but the fatherly and gracious will of God." (Luther)

As the malefactor, the highwayman who was crucified with Him, was the first evangelist of the cross of Christ, so Mary Magdalene, once possessed by devils, became the first evangelist of the resurrection. Neither

Peter nor John, but this woman with a questionable past became the first evangelist. She is permitted to bring the name "Brother" to the terrified disciples. For the risen Lord Himself "makes a preacher of her that she must be a master and teacher of the dear apostles." (Luther)

CHAPTER X

The Second Word of the Risen Lord

Jesus Himself drew near and went with them. But their eyes were holden that they should not know Him. And He said unto them, What manner of communications are these that ye have one to another as ye walk and are sad? And the one of them, whose name was Cleopas, answering, said unto Him: Art thou only a stranger in Jerusalem and hast not known the things which are come to pass there in these days? And He said unto them, What things? And they said unto Him: Concerning Jesus of Nazareth, which was a prophet mighty in deed and word before God and all the people, and how the chief priests and our rulers delivered Him to be condemned to death and have crucified Him. But we trusted that it had been He which should have redeemed Israel; and beside all this, today is the third day since these things were done. Yea, and certain women also of our company made us astonished, which were early at the sepulcher; and when they found not His body, they came, saying, that they had also seen a vision of angels which said that He was alive. And certain of them which were with us went to the sepulcher and found it even so as the women had said; but Him they saw not. Then He said unto them: O fools and slow of heart to believe all that the prophets have spoken; ought not Christ

to have suffered these things and to enter into His glory?
And beginning at Moses and all the prophets, He expounded
unto them in all the Scriptures the things concerning Himself.
And they drew nigh unto the village whither they went; and
He made as though He would have gone further. But they
constrained Him, saying: Abide with us; for it is toward
evening, and the day is far spent. And He went in to tarry
with them. And it came to pass, as He sat at meat with them,
He took bread, and blessed it, and brake, and gave to them.
And their eyes were opened, and they knew Him; and He
vanished out of their sight. And they said one to another,
Did not our heart burn within us while He talked with us
by the way and while He opened to us the Scriptures?
(Luke 24:15-32)

HOW MUCH these two disciples know who are running
away from the place of the grimmest catastrophe of
their life, the place where their Master was crucified!
They forsake the communion of the apostles and the
women because in their aching hearts everything has
collapsed!

They know about Jesus, the Prophet "mighty in
deed and word before God and all the people," and
they saw His cross, prepared by the chief priests and
rulers. But they do not believe that this very death
on the cross is the greatest deed and the sweetest sermon
of this Prophet. They know that Israel is to be redeemed and had expected this of their Master. But
they do not believe that this redemption has already
been accomplished by the Master's gruesome death.
They know about the empty tomb and have heard the
report of the resurrection. But they cannot comprehend

that Jesus is risen indeed. They know about every deed that guarantees their redemption and gives them reason to break forth in joyful song. But their knowledge consists of fragments that don't fit together but stand disjointed beside and against one another. They do not know about the unity of the cross and the resurrection.

So they walk with the risen Lord, but they see only a stranger. Him who knows all, they regard as ignorant. Him who loves them most sincerely they believe to be indifferent. He who is very close to them seems far away. He who has found them seems entirely lost to them. They see the stranger walk with them and hear Him speak, but they do not recognize in Him the crucified Lord. All of their knowledge about Jesus' deed and word "lies in their heart altogether inactive, cold, and idle, just like an empty husk without sap and strength, neither profiting nor helping, neither strengthening nor improving them" (Luther). "Their eyes were holden."

In His goodness the risen Lord reproves the two men, not for failing to recognize Him or for failing to trust in His resurrection — "O fools and slow of heart to believe all that the prophets have spoken" — He reproves them for not believing the Word of Scripture, the Word of the Old Testament.

In contrast to the disciples the Lord begins not with what they experienced and what they know but with the Word of Scripture. "And beginning at Moses and all the prophets, He expounded unto them in all the Scriptures the things concerning Himself." We cannot appreciate how remarkable this procedure really was. It is significant that Luke does not mention any specific Old Testament passages which Jesus interpreted. The big concern is "all." All the prophets speak by the mouth of Jesus; all the Scriptures that speak of Him Jesus explains; all that the prophets have spoken should be believed. The one great fact to which all Old Testament Scriptures bear witness is the great "must," laid down by God, which combines Christ's suffering and glory, cross and resurrection, into an inseparable unity. "Ought not Christ to have suffered these things and to enter into His glory?" Christ cannot be Lord without suffering; He cannot suffer without entering into His glory. If He had not been crucified, He would be exposed as a deceiver. But because He has been crucified, He must also rise. God has ordained this "must." God remains faithful and keeps His promises. He cannot lie.

Men have speculated again and again as to which passages of the Old Testament were mentioned and explained by Christ. If we pursue the interpretation of this Easter text through church history, we run into the story of a great and varied "second guessing" (Luther). Was it Psalm 16: "Thou wilt not leave My soul in hell; neither wilt Thou suffer Thine Holy One to see corruption" (verse 10; cf. Acts 2:27)? Was it Psalm 8: "Thou hast made Him a little lower than the angels and hast crowned Him with glory and honor" (verse 5 or Heb. 2:7)? Or Psalm 110: "The

Lord saith unto my Lord, Sit Thou at My right hand until I make Thine enemies Thy footstool" (verse 1 or Heb. 10:12)? Was it Isaiah 53: "Yet it pleased the Lord to bruise Him; He hath put Him to grief; when Thou shalt make His soul an offering for sin, He shall see His seed, He shall prolong His days" (verse 10)? Or Hosea 6: "After two days will He revive us; in the third day He will raise us up, and we shall live in His sight" (verse 2)? Or Genesis 3, the curse of God pronounced upon the serpent: The Son of the woman "shall bruise thy head, and thou shalt bruise His heel" (verse 15)? Thus we could keep on asking and follow up all the Old Testament passages which the New Testament quotes and identifies as testimony of the suffering and resurrection of Christ. And in fact these Old Testament words have always been considered in the interpretation of the Emmaus story.

But whoever thinks only of individual passages will not recognize the great, revolutionary event that occurred in Emmaus. It is no accident that Luke does not mention the passages which Jesus interprets. The interpretation by the risen Lord rather opens the Old Testament as a whole. The risen Lord tears away the veil over the Old Testament as a whole and reveals the all-embracing sweep of its glory. The risen Lord's interpretation of Scripture is a miracle as is the resurrection itself. He removes the veil from the Testament whose glory, if it had not been hidden till then, would have killed man. But this is the glory of the Old

Testament that it confesses the Christ who must be crucified by man and is exalted by God to be the Lord.

This the Old Testament confesses in all its books, indeed, in all its passages. Every individual passage can be nothing else than a reference to the fact that the crucified and risen Lord is the premise and the goal whenever the Holy God speaks to the sinner. Nothing else is intended by the apparently accidental manner with which the New Testament now quotes a word spoken to David, to Solomon, now a word about man in general, now a lament of the church as a testimony concerning Christ. The crucified and risen Lord is the premise and the goal of each king, priest, and prophet in the Old Covenant. It is the premise and the goal of every lamentation and every hymn of praise which Israel uttered before the face of God. In fact, it is the premise and the goal of every human existence in this world of sin and death. The holy God would have hurled the sinner to bits and crushed him with His angry silence if from the beginning His dear Son had not stood before Him with His intercession. From the beginning the sinner remained alive only because of the future new life of the risen Lord. The entire Old Testament is a hymn of praise to the glory of Jesus Christ.

To the disciples of all ages the risen Lord says: O fools and slow of heart, face the Word of the Old Testament that you may know Me and your sorrow may be transformed into joy! Believe what is said there, that you may be set free of your folly! In your discussions among yourselves you remain only fools who continue to brood even though all your questions have already been answered. The conversations that you have, the one with the other and each one with himself, are only "on the way," as a man on an outing is on the way and returns to the house he left in the morning. If you do not subject your thinking to the word of the Old Testament, all your thoughts must magnify the question from which they started into boundless proportions. If you do not believe Moses and the prophets, you will not recognize any act of God that happens before your very eyes, but you will constantly confuse God and the devil, heaven and hell, death and life, as if you were blind.

Though Christ removes the veil from the Scripture for the disciples on their way to Emmaus, they do not recognize Him. Even though He who Himself is the Word proclaims the Word of the Old Testament to them, the risen Lord still is hidden from them. The fact that they do not recognize the risen Lord shows that in spite of Christ's explanation they still do not believe the Word of the prophets. "The veil is upon their heart" (2 Cor. 3:15). For whoever does not believe the Word of Scripture does not know the risen Lord; and whoever does not recognize the risen Lord does not believe the Word of Scripture.

Thus the disciples as blind men ask the Lord of the world to be their guest. They invite Him as the stranger who is not at home in this country. Prompted by a yearning hidden from themselves, they take pity on Him who on the cross had pity on them and in His great mercy now follows them and calls them. What fools we are! We treat Him as a guest, though we live only as His guests; we look upon Him as a stranger who has purchased us to be His own. But Christ, also as the risen and exalted Lord, is not ashamed to be lowly and to enter into His own country as a guest.

"And it came to pass, as He sat at meat with them, He took bread, and blessed it, and brake, and gave to them. And their eyes were opened, and they knew Him." They had not recognized the risen Lord when they first saw Him or when He explained the Scriptures to them. Whoever wants to have the resurrection without the cross will not know the risen Lord. And whoever searches the Scriptures without recognizing the crucified Lord as the risen Lord will in spite of Scripture remain in his blindness. The risen Lord made Himself known to the two disciples by showing Himself to be the Lord who with them went to the cross. As He takes the bread, blesses it, and gives it to them, as He had done it daily, as He had, in fact, done in the evening before His death, He proves Himself to be the very same One who once and again now walked with them, who once and again now taught them, who loved them then and loves them now. By thanking and giving, the Guest becomes the Host, and He who received becomes the One who makes the giver rich.

He does not become this host only now, however, but He reveals Himself as the One who formerly made them rich and now will make them much richer.

The miracle of all miracles, the wisdom of all wisdom, and the key of all keys is this, that Christ was victorious as He died, that He was exalted as the cross was lifted up, and that He stooped down as He rose, that He at once gave Himself as another gift after He had again taken up His life in the tomb of death. The necessary unity of Christ's suffering and glory, the victory on the cross and the condescension in the resurrection, this is the greatest wisdom. Whoever does not know the crucified Lord does not know the risen Lord. And whoever does not know the risen Lord does not know the crucified Lord. None of the seven words on the cross would be a comfort if the crucified Lord had not risen. And none of the words of the risen Lord would be a comfort if they were not spoken to us by the crucified Lord.

Only now, after the eyes of the disciples had been opened to recognize Jesus, do they realize that He has removed the veil from Scripture, has "opened" Scripture to them. It is not a mere coincidence that Luke in his report uses the same word for the opening of the eyes to see the risen Lord and the opening of Scripture by Him. For both are one and the same act. As they recognize the risen Lord, who then immediately vanished out of their sight, they recognize the glory of the Old Testament forever.

The Old Testament is not solved for anybody except by faith in the crucified and risen Lord, and the crucified and risen Lord is not revealed to anybody without the Old Testament. Whoever believes in the victory of the crucified Lord in His resurrection can more easily do without the Scripture of the New Testament than without the Scripture of the Old Testament. For "the New Testament is nothing else but an opening and revelation of the Old Testament." "If I had the Holy Spirit, I, too, could make a New Testament out of the passages of the Old Testament if it had not already been done." (Luther)

CHAPTER XI

The Third Word of the Risen Lord

And as they thus spake, Jesus Himself stood in the midst of them and saith unto them, Peace be unto you. But they were terrified and affrighted and supposed that they had seen a spirit. And He said unto them: Why are ye troubled? And why do thoughts arise in your hearts? Behold My hands and My feet, that it is I Myself; handle Me and see; for a spirit hath not flesh and bones, as ye see Me have. And when He had thus spoken, He showed them His hands and His feet. And while they yet believed not for joy and wondered, He said unto them, Have ye here any meat? And they gave Him a piece of a broiled fish and of an honeycomb. And He took it and did eat before them. (Luke 24:36-43)

JUST WHAT does this mean: The crucified Lord is risen, He is risen indeed? Faced with this proclamation, men have from the beginning tried various means of escape. Yes, even when facing the risen Lord Himself, man resists with the strangest theories just to evade this miracle, which alone gives us life.

Is He who appears a specter? Were the disciples so far wrong when they "supposed that they had seen

71

a spirit"? If Satan can camouflage himself as an angel of light (2 Cor. 2:14), then he can create the illusion of being Christ Himself. His work is the work of Lucifer, who seems to be bringing light, though Jesus Christ alone is "the Light which lighteth every man."

Or are the appearances of the Crucified One apparitions produced by the longing of the tortured hearts of the women and disciples? Nothing suggests itself more readily — in this point liberal theology was right — than to assume that when a person speaks of appearances they are only subjective experiences of visions. Who knows his heart and the hidden escape mechanism of his soul, which at any cost would transform despair into joy and disappointment into triumph so that we are able to live even if only by deceiving ourselves?

The resurrected Lord Himself takes an opposing stand to all this as He says, "Behold My hands and My feet, that it is I Myself." He responds by offering Himself to the eye and demands that the eye be realistic.

One could continue to ask: Is it not perhaps Jesus' spirit rushing forward once more to the circle of His friends from the distant realm of death, becoming visible to them and speaking to them? But He says: "Handle Me and see, for a spirit hath not flesh and bones, as ye see Me have."

Or has not perhaps the spirit of Jesus merely assumed a bodily appearance in order to be visible? Has He perhaps merely disguised Himself with flesh and blood in order to comfort and restore by this sign? No, He offers to the touch the same body which hung dead on the cross, for He shows them the scars in His hands and feet. He offers for inspection and handling the same body which lay dead in the grave, for the grave is empty. And who could have stolen the body, since the grave had been sealed? Or how could His body not have been a corpse, since it had been opened with a spear and blood and water came out of it?

"It is I Myself," that is: It is I entirely, neither spirit nor body, but spirit in the body. A spirit without a body is nakedness, nothingness, and deadness. A body without a spirit is a corpse, decay, and dust. But Jesus Christ is risen from the dead on the third day. He is risen indeed, He is risen bodily. The grave was empty.

What does this mean: He is risen bodily?

The body of the risen Lord is not like the body which walked from the manger to the cross. Suddenly the risen Lord stands in the midst of the disciples "before they could have noticed Him coming" (Bengel); therefore they were terrified (verses 36 ff.). Even through closed doors the risen Lord steps into their midst and proclaims His greeting of peace (John 20: 19, 26). Entering mysteriously and again disappearing just as mysteriously, not immediately recognizable and yet recognized beyond the shadow of a doubt, hidden in the resurrection body and yet in the same body as manifest as never before, intimate and yet distant — thus the risen Lord walks the earth until He bodily

73

ascends to heaven. His body is different from an earthly body.

At the same time it is true that the body of the risen Lord is the same body which walked from the manger to the cross. He bears the prints of the crucifixion in His hands and His feet and shows the gash of the spear. But the grave was empty. This identity cannot be taken seriously enough. It is the same beaten, tortured, and disfigured body which only three days ago hung on the cross and now is risen in glory. "He remains the same and yet does not return to the former mode of life, but has become new. He controls space, as we do not control it; He is here and there as He wills. He passes through what is impenetrable for us and therefore stands in an altogether different relationship to our nature than we do. And yet He remains a bodily being, and what He had in His body before dying continues to live in Him. We face a miracle which is completely unfathomable for us." (Schlatter)

We ask again, What is the meaning of: The crucified Lord is risen bodily?

The resurrection of Jesus is a phenomenon different from the raising of the young man at Nain and of Lazarus in Bethany. Jesus was not only raised as Lazarus and the young man were raised, but unlike these two He also rose of His own power. "He took up His life again." But if we saw only this difference, we would still misunderstand the resurrection of Jesus. For the resurrection of Lazarus and of the others was

74

a continuation of the earthly life, a continuation of a life in death, a raising for another death. But the resurrection of Jesus ends death as well as the life in death. It is definitely not the continuation of earthly life. It is a promoting to a different life, not the raising of the earthly body to continue the old life but the resurrection of the spiritual body for life everlasting.

The difference between the resurrection of Lazarus and of Christ consists in this, "that Christ, being raised from the dead, dieth no more; death hath no more dominion over Him. For in that He died, He died unto sin once; but in that He liveth, He liveth unto God" (Rom. 6:9, 10). The raising of the son of the widow at Nain and of the brother of Mary and Martha at Bethany are only signs pointing to the resurrection of Jesus Christ. Their life from their rising to their second death are mere signs pointing to the entirely different, eternal life of the risen, eternal Son, our first-born Brother. The resurrections before the resurrection of Jesus are as different from it as the Old Testament king is different from the King of Kings, the only Anointed One, Jesus Christ, even though the Old Testament office of king was a sign pointing to the coming Christ. As Jesus Christ is a king, priest, and prophet different from all the kings, priests, and prophets before Him, so His risen bodily existence is different from that of all other earthly bodies, different also from the bodily existence of the people whom He had previously healed and snatched from death.

At the same time this is true: the raising of Jesus, like that of Lazarus and the young man, is a raising from the dead. And, again, in the raising of Jesus, as in that of Lazarus and the young man, there is raised the same body which formerly walked on the earth and then fell to the earth as a corpse.

We dare not speak of the resurrection of Jesus Christ except in two different statements whose harmony cannot be made reasonable: The body of the risen Lord is different from His earthly body and all earthly bodies, and yet it is His risen earthly body. The manner of this unity is God's very own mystery. This identity with all its differences can only be believed, but not described. Whoever would say more than this — for instance, of what kind of material this new body consists, why the wounds still remain — will only say less. But whoever would say less — who with ancient interpreters would interpret "flesh and bones" allegorically as absence and fullness of power, weakness and strength, of Jesus — will at once no longer be speaking of the risen Lord.

The crucified Christ rose bodily, and as such He is the new Man, the second Man. The risen Lord is different from us sinners after the Fall, different also from Adam before the Fall. He is the other, the second Adam. "And so it is written: The first man, Adam, was made a living soul; the last Adam was made a quickening spirit. . . ." The first man is of the earth, earthy; the second Man is the Lord from heaven"

(1 Cor. 15:45, 47). The first man was created by God to live eternally in the obedience of faith. Jesus Christ, however, the other Man, is the first to attain this life by believing and being obedient unto death. All before Him failed to reach this life because they all sinned against God. They all remained in the earthly sphere from which God took their bodies, and they were held fast there as sinners by death and the devil and were sealed in their curse.

But Jesus Christ did not overcome the sinners and the world to leave them behind. He did not rise only for Himself. He did not clutch His own resurrection firmly in His hands as if it were a prize. No sooner had He escaped death than the Lord turned to those who had killed and forsaken Him in death. No sooner had He frustrated the world and its enmity than the risen Lord extended His hands to offer Himself and His resurrection to the world.

The resurrection of Jesus is the beginning of many new men, the beginning of a new human race. The human race, subjected to death by sin, receives life through the risen Lord. The bodies which here on earth decay shall rise through Him in the likeness of His glorified body. We must be careful not to water down the promise of life. Not only is this promise another term for the word of forgiveness, but to those who believe it the life in Christ's new heavenly bodily existence is also given. Hear this message, particularly you who are miserable, weak, and ill, groaning under the burden of your body. Believe this message, you who "do not count," who are homely and disfigured, who feel that your body is a constant disgrace before the whole world. Christ is comfort and salvation even for your body.

The resurrection of Jesus Christ is at the same time the beginning of a new world. As the first Adam was ordained to be the lord of the first earth so the second Adam was ordained to be the Lord of the new earth. As Adam's deed was to make a decision for a world so Christ's deed is the decision for a new world. Jesus Christ is the great turning point not only for all mankind but also for all creation. From His birth onward His way is certified not only by men but also by angels, even by the star of Bethlehem. And, again, not only men are affected by His death but also the earth that shakes, the rocks that split, and the sun that loses its brightness. All of them are affected by the resurrection of Jesus. As the fate of the first world was decided by Adam's deed so the beginning of a new world, the founding of a new heaven and a new earth, was decided by the deed of Christ. As the first creation was delivered into the dominion of the devil and of death by Adam's sin, so the liberated, new creation was called up by the obedience and the resurrection of Jesus Christ. When He returns, the risen Lord will replace the crumbling earth and the fading stars with the new earth and the new heaven. As the men who then arise are the same who were once created by God and then fell into death and vanity through their own fault so the new earth which then will come is the same earth which was created by God and then because of sin was subjected to the curse. But this same earth will be completely new.

The resurrected Lord does not keep His resurrection as a prize for Himself. This is shown by the fact that He appeared to men to have them look at, touch, and ask Him. This is shown by the fact that He calls them brethren in a sense which includes life and death. This turning of the risen Lord to fallen creation finds its most objective expression in His question, "Have ye here any meat?" And He not only asked but also "took it and did eat before them," though He surely did not need this food. This eating of the risen Lord is recorded with stark realism, and His presence at a meal of His disciples is also reported elsewhere. Blessed is he who is not offended at the reality of this eating! The reality of this eating is the reality of grace. So low stoops the risen Lord to men, who are but dust and ashes. Christ, the new Man, is not ashamed to eat with men of the old world the products of the old world. He receives the old creation into His new life. He draws it after Him.

CHAPTER XII

The Fourth Word of the Risen Lord

But Thomas, one of the twelve, called Didymus, was not with them when Jesus came. The other disciples therefore said unto him, We have seen the Lord. But he said unto them: Except I shall see in His hands the print of the nails, and put my finger into the print of the nails, and thrust my hand into His side, I will not believe. And after eight days again His disciples were within and Thomas with them; then came Jesus, the doors being shut, and stood in the midst and said, Peace be unto you. Then saith He to Thomas: Reach hither thy finger, and behold My hands; and reach hither thy hand, and thrust it into My side; and be not faithless, but believing. And Thomas answered and said unto Him, My Lord and my God. Jesus saith unto him: Thomas, because thou hast seen Me, thou hast believed; blessed are they that have not seen and yet have believed. (John 20:24-29)

AGAIN THE RISEN LORD appears in the circle of His disciples. Great is the condescension with which He again lets Himself be seen and even touched. But even greater is the condescension with which He at the same time crosses out both seeing and touching. For only as

80

Christ's Word takes away the importance of sight is the entire resurrection of Jesus Christ given to us who do not see Him. This devaluation of seeing with our own eyes makes the risen Lord real, true, and close to us.

Thomas had heard the disciples declare, "We have seen the Lord." They probably also told him that the grave was found empty and what the angels had proclaimed at the grave. He surely also heard what the risen Lord had told the terrified and blind women and disciples. Thus he is in the same position as we who have not seen the risen Lord, but hear about His resurrection.

Thomas "does not say, When I see Him, I shall believe, but only, Unless I shall see Him, I shall not believe. He does not think that he will see Him, even though the others declare that they have seen Him" (Bengel). He is not a man of little faith, but a man of no faith. He is not merely unsure and doubtful, but determined in his skeptical, dejected stubbornness. If the others have seen the risen Lord, he wants to see and touch Him. He wants to satisfy the slowest of all senses, the sense of touch. He wants this, and yet at the same time he doesn't want it, because he doesn't count on the fulfillment of his wish. If the others have seen the hands of the risen Lord, he wants to see and touch also His body, whose side was pierced by a spear. His passion centers in the wound which proves death. Thereby he presents an ultimatum in the most real sense. Barricaded behind rejection and stubbornness, he declares war on the risen Lord: "Except I shall see in His hands the print of the nails . . . and thrust my hand into His side, I will not believe."

Now let us not say, This is a stubbornness which still is ready to have something to do with Christ. No, there is no glory here. Nor let us offer the excuse: Thomas remained in the circle of the disciples and waited day after day. There is a waiting which does not want to receive, but only to show that it is right and that others are wrong. "Thomas' stubbornness is surprising, indeed, monstrous." He is "not only stubborn but also arrogant and insulting toward Christ" (Calvin). He acts as do the people who say: "If there is a God, let Him help me; if I receive help, then there is a God." Such talk is tempting and blaspheming God.

It is inconceivably great condescension on the part of the risen Lord to come to this man. The man who had threatened war Christ greets with "Peace be unto you." Peace be unto you who have already begun the war against Me. The risen Lord not only wishes Thomas this peace, but brings it to him: "Reach hither thy finger, and behold My hands; and reach hither thy hand, and thrust it into My side." The risen Lord brings peace by submitting to the stubbornness of Thomas, by exposing Himself to his insult, by fulfilling his haughty terms of peace. In His message to Thomas the Lord repeats the demands of Thomas word for word as a challenge accepted. Not one demand remains unfulfilled. Not a single counterdemand is added. Only a request follows: "Be not faithless, but believing," do not resist, but receive the gift, do not demand, but take.

It is overwhelming that the risen Lord permits Himself to be overwhelmed. It is disarming that Christ lays down all arms and surrenders to our stubbornness. The risen Victor, capitulating before the ultimatum of a sinner who is a slave of death — that defeats us, throws us to the ground, onto our knees. We may imagine that we are able to contradict the greatness of God, but the humility of God destroys our resistance. Thus in a moment Christ turns foes into friends, deniers into confessors, unbelievers into believers. With one stroke Thomas reaches the climax of faith and surpasses by far all other disciples. By Christ's humility this development became an event which older exegetes found foreshadowed already in Thomas' name: " 'Didymus' means 'twin' because of the cleft heart, but 'Thomas' means 'abyss,' because with firm faith he penetrated the height of deity." (Alcuin)

Overwhelmed by Him who unresistingly lets Himself be overwhelmed, Thomas can only be consumed with shame, and of his own accord he foregoes the conditions he has made. He believes even before he touches the risen Lord. Even though he had wanted to be convinced only as he saw and touched, he is convinced by sight alone and foregoes the opportunity to touch the body of Christ.

This is adoration and thanks. This is the greatest

praise. In fact, this waiving of the privilege by the most stubborn opponent becomes perhaps the most comprehensive confession ever offered to Christ by a disciple: "My Lord and my God." These words Thomas speaks not to the distant God in heaven, but he addresses the risen Lord standing before him on this earth. He is the Lord, and He is God. God, the Lord Himself, became man in His Son. God, the Lord Himself, suffered on the cross for us. Again, the man Jesus is God, the Lord, who revealed Himself in the Old Testament. The appearance of Jesus is the appearance of God: "He that hath seen Me hath seen the Father" (John 14:9). The word of Jesus is God's Word; more, Jesus is the one Word of whom the opening of John's Gospel testifies: "The Word was with God, and the Word was God" (John 1:1). This Son of Man, Jesus, who is God the Lord from eternity, who was Lord also in His humiliation, has been exalted to be Lord in His resurrection. With the cry "My Lord and my God" Thomas also claims everything done on the cross as having been done for him; and everything that the risen Lord is and does he calls his own. For the risen Lord is not Lord for Himself, but Lord for me, my Lord, that is, my Brother.

Is this word of Thomas a confession? Is it not perhaps only an indication of the overcharged hour, an outburst of the agony and yearning hidden in his stubbornness? Is not this word perhaps closer to stubbornness than appears on the surface? Is it not perhaps only a defense mechanism and an expression which man devises for himself?

True, as a purely human word Thomas' word can be no more. But the risen Lord fashions it into something else. He Himself makes of it a confession of faith by His response, "Because thou hast seen Me, thou hast believed." No one confesses Christ on the basis of words formed by himself. We become confessors when Christ confesses Himself to be ours and acknowledges our thoughts and prattle by saying, Yes, you believe. The yes of Christ leads to this word of Thomas, a glory which confirms the glory of God. The yes of Christ makes this word of Thomas perhaps the greatest homage ever offered by a disciple. Before this no one had expressed the mystery of Jesus Christ so clearly.

Thus the risen Lord in one moment transforms the unbelieving stubborn man into a teacher of the church, which at all times has repeated and always will repeat His confession. I believe "in one Lord Jesus Christ, the only-begotten Son of God . . . God of God, Light of Light, very God of very God" (Nicene Creed). "We confess one only Son, our Lord Jesus Christ . . . perfect in deity and perfect in humanity, that the same is true God and true man" (Chalcedon). "I believe that Jesus Christ, true God, begotten of the Father from eternity, and also true man, born of the Virgin Mary, is my Lord." (Luther's Small Catechism)

Even greater than the condescension with which

the risen Lord comes to Thomas and submits to his look and his touch is the mercy with which He minimizes such sight and touch as He says, "Blessed are they that have not seen and yet have believed." Not the fact of the resurrection but this seeing of the risen Lord is crossed out. Not the testimony of the resurrection but human sensation is thereby made unimportant. We are to believe the testimony as we believe the risen Lord Himself. True faith is the faith which never laid eyes on the risen Lord.

"Blessed are they that have not seen and yet have believed." This beatitude doesn't really apply to Thomas, for he believed because he saw. Strictly speaking, it doesn't apply to any of the apostles, for the Lord did appear to them. This word moves swiftly on. "Blessed are you who after His ascension no longer see Him and yet believe. The last word of the risen Lord is meant for us. We have the advantage of this beatitude. It "raises the communion of believers above the apostles. God's Word does not sink, it rises" (Schlatter). Here there is no advantage for the apostles, no disadvantage for us. It is not an advantage to see the risen Lord, but to hear the message: He is risen indeed. It is not an advantage to have looked into the empty grave, but to believe the message: the grave was empty. "If then someone should say: If I had only lived in those times and had seen Christ perform miracles, let him remember, Blessed are they that have not seen, and yet have believed." (Chrysostom)

We believe even while we doubt. We hope even while we are downcast and constantly see more hopelessness. We are still sad, fearful, and discouraged. But when we shall one day rise, we shall remember with the joyous laughter of Easter the folly which still wept where there was every reason for joy and which was still stubborn where, in spite of our stubbornness, we were already surrounded and shielded by the death and life of Christ.

Even greater than the great condescension with which He came to Thomas is the condescension with which He makes this appearance in the flesh of little value. By devaluing completely everything that He permits Thomas, He permits all succeeding generations to cling to Him: He is risen not for Thomas only but for all of you. He offers Himself not only to the disciples but also to you. All of you are invited to believe. Blessed are you who believe.

CHAPTER XIII

The Fifth Word of the Risen Lord

So when they had dined, Jesus saith to Simon Peter: Simon, son of Jonas, lovest thou Me more than these? He saith unto Him, Yea, Lord, Thou knowest that I love Thee. He saith unto him, Feed My lambs. He saith to him again the second time, Simon, son of Jonas, lovest thou Me? He saith unto Him, Yea, Lord, Thou knowest that I love Thee. He saith unto him, Feed My sheep. He saith unto him the third time, Simon, son of Jonas, lovest thou Me? Peter was grieved because He said unto him the third time, Lovest thou Me? And he said unto Him: Lord, Thou knowest all things; Thou knowest that I love Thee. Jesus saith unto Him, Feed My sheep. Verily, verily, I say unto thee, When thou wast young, thou girdedst thyself and walkedst whither thou wouldest; but when thou shalt be old, thou shalt stretch forth thy hands, and another shall gird thee and carry thee whither thou wouldest not. This spake He, signifying by what death he should glorify God. And when He had spoken this, He saith unto him, Follow Me. (John 21:15-19)

HERE the risen Lord speaks to the disciple who had denied Him three times, who had run away even though he had declared himself willing to die for Jesus (John

88

13:37), who had fled in terror from the disgrace of the cross though he had promised, "Though all men shall be offended because of Thee, yet will I never be offended" (Matt. 26:33). The risen Lord speaks to this man in a manner which utterly disconcerts us. If we try to understand the words of the risen Lord to Peter in the light of the ordinary understanding of Law and Gospel, if we expect to find in them at least an assurance of forgiveness, we are at first puzzled. For the message of the risen Lord does not mention the sin of Peter. It does not ask, What have you done? It does not urge: Repent. Nor does the word of the risen Lord command him: Commit yourself to grace, believe in forgiveness. Indeed, it does not even say: I forgive you. No, the forgiveness of the risen Lord is so grand and overwhelming that He does not even speak of forgiveness. To say, "I forgive you," would have been a reminder of the sin he had committed. But the reality of this forgiveness steps across all that has happened and all pious expectations.

The yes which Jesus expects of Peter is not the yes that confesses the past, but the yes of the present. It is not the retrospective yes of confession — Yes, I have denied Thee; yes, I am unworthy of Thy love — but the yes of present love: Yes, I love Thee, and I'll not leave Thee. The past is swallowed up by the fact of the resurrection. This yes Peter offers in deepest fear and shame, "Lord, Thou knowest that I love Thee." He cannot point to any proof of his love; he can only point to the knowledge of Jesus, in which even the longing to love and even the tears of the denier are recorded. And who can know about his own love in any other way than by knowing that in spite of our sins we are sheltered as loving ones in Jesus, who knows us. "Lord, Thou knowest all things; Thou knowest that I love Thee."

But isn't this a word of judgment when the risen Lord asks, Lovest thou Me more than these? Isn't this "more," which raises Peter above the other disciples, a reminder of his presumptuous promise? Is it not a call to repentance when the Lord three times questions him who had three times denied Him? Doesn't the threefold question recall the threefold guilt? Isn't the denier stripped of all trustworthiness when for the third time the question no longer concerns love, but only the modest reality of his affection and friendship, which was all that Peter in all his replies had dared to claim?

But the question repeated three times simply serves to introduce the forgiveness repeated three times. And the forgiveness is so complete and removes and forgets the past so completely that the word "forgiveness" is not even mentioned, but the fallen apostle is newly commissioned three times as an apostle: "Feed My lambs." "Feed My sheep." "Feed My sheep." This commission is forgiveness. This assignment to service is grace. The office of the shepherd, the office of proclaiming the Gospel, is not a law imposed upon the sinner that he may perish in his sins, but is a gift, peace, joy, and salvation. Therefore each of the three questions which introduce the commissioning of Peter is not so much a challenge and a test as rather a blessing.

But even apart from these words addressed to Peter, the appearances of the risen Lord between Easter and Ascension are in every instance real forgiveness for those to whom the Lord appears. For they reveal the fact that God has accepted the sacrifice on the cross and has really reconciled the sinners with Himself. The resurrection of Jesus is the seal and the proclamation of the fact that the crucified Christ, and He alone, died sinless for the sins of the others. The risen Lord comes to all the disciples and women to whom He appears as the Forgiver whose forgiveness is so great and overwhelming that He doesn't even say, I forgive you. In that He reproaches none of them for their flight, their unbelief, and their despair on Calvary, His greeting, questions, and command are in every case superabundant mercy.

Who is it that commands Peter, "Feed My sheep"? This is the voice of the Good Shepherd. Jesus Christ is the one Shepherd, and He remains the Shepherd, the Chief Shepherd of His flock.

To whom does Jesus Christ speak? He tells a member of His flock, "Feed My sheep," be a member of the flock and a shepherd of the flock at the same time, be an image of the Good Shepherd under the Good Shepherd. If Peter is commissioned a shepherd as an image of the one Shepherd Jesus Christ, then also his

91

activity is to be an image of the activity of Jesus. As Jesus leads the flock as a whole and tenderly cares for it, so Peter is now to lead it. As Jesus has pity on every little lamb and especially on the weak, so Peter is to guard and foster all members of the flock and especially those whom the world has given up as unfit to live. As Jesus knew about sheep who belonged to His flock even when they were not yet added to the flock, so Peter is to follow up the strayed sheep and bring them in that there may be one flock and one Shepherd. As the risen Lord comforts Peter, so Peter should comfort the others. He also is to know about the love of the other ones, though they may not be aware of it now and though their love does not manifest itself in any deeds. After all, Jesus knew about Peter's love when he denied Him.

Thus Peter is to be a shepherd in the place of the one Shepherd. Jesus, the Lord, "loves His flock, and He entrusts it to him who loves Him" (Bengel). Peter is to feed Jesus' sheep in Jesus' place. But the sheep remain Jesus' sheep. They do not become Peter's sheep. The commission reads, "Feed My sheep." "Feed My sheep as Mine, not as yours; seek My glory in them, not yours; My kingdom, not yours; My wealth, not yours." (Augustine)

Again we must ask, Who is it that commands Peter to be a shepherd? And now we must answer, "The Lamb of God, which taketh away the sin of the world" (John 1:29), the Lamb that was slaughtered and slain.

The word with which the risen Lord designates and entrusts the members of His flock (John 21:16) is the same as designates the risen Lord Himself. Before the throne of God the angels and the elders and the beasts adore and praise Him as "the Lamb that was slain" (Rev. 5:12). The Lamb that was slain and still lives, that died without honor and to whom alone honor is due, commands, "Feed My lambs."

When the Lamb installs Peter as shepherd, there takes place an exchange which is inconceivably great and at the same time most deeply humbling. The Good Shepherd becomes the Lamb, and one of His lambs becomes a shepherd. As in the incarnation, the Lord God became a servant, and we slaves became lords — what an exchange! — just as the righteous Christ is made to be sin by God and we sinners are made to be righteousness in Him, as the innocent Christ was condemned on the cross that we sinners might be acquitted in Him, so the Good Shepherd was slain as a lamb, but Peter, a member of His flock, was installed as shepherd. Peter the shepherd substituting for Jesus Christ requires Jesus Christ the Lamb substituting for Peter. There is no substitution in the congregation of Jesus Christ except the exchange of Christ with it.

This exchange again impresses the truth: Feed, that is, proceed from Him who died on the cross for you, and lead the others to Him who died for them. Feed, that is, proceed from the superabundant forgiveness of the resurrection, and tenderly invite people by praising and promising forgiveness. Comfort as the Lamb that was slain comforted His own after His resurrection.

This exchange has a fixed order. As the exchange between the Lord God and us, His servants, between the sinless Son and us, the sinners, so also this exchange between the Shepherd and us, the members of His flock, is not reversible, but has its fixed order. Peter is shepherd, because Jesus was slain for him as the Lamb, but Jesus was not to be Shepherd because Peter died for Him. The arrogance of Peter was this, that he wanted to die before Jesus died. He wanted to die before Jesus for Jesus. It was this very resolution that led to the denial. To resolve to die for Jesus before Jesus' death is "to gird oneself," "to walk whither one would." Before another could die for Jesus, Jesus had to die first. First Jesus had to die for those who were to give their life for Him. But now He died and rose again. "Now it is time, Peter, that you do not fear death, since He is living whom you mourned as dead and whom in your earthly love you wanted to keep from dying for us. You dared to go before the Leader; therefore you trembled in the presence of those who persecuted Him. Now since the ransom has been paid, now it is time for you to follow Him who paid the ransom, and follow Him all the way to death on the cross." (Augustine)

This order of succession is fixed by God. It is the order of following after. Not the sinner who needs to be freed dare die for the Liberator; but being freed by the death of the Liberator, the sinner is to praise

94

the Liberator by following after Him until death. A dying for Jesus before Jesus died would not glorify God's deed but be an attempt to prevent it. "Put up again thy sword into his place" (Matt. 26:52). Only a dying that follows Jesus is a dying for Jesus and glorifies God.

We do not decide to die in this way, but if it comes, we are led into it. We do not dare and seek such a death, but we are ready for it if the situation arises. We do not follow Jesus by a decision of our own, but by God's decision and .Christ's command, Follow after Me. As an old man does not walk alone, but is led by another as he walks and extends his arm in a plea for assistance; as a condemned man drags his cross to the place of execution not free but tied to the beams of the cross and thus is taken where he does not want to go, so the way of following Jesus is the way of being led and overcome. But to be called by Christ is a gift, and to be overcome by Christ is freedom, and to die with Christ is life.

CHAPTER XIV

The Sixth Word of the Risen Lord

Then said Jesus to them again: Peace be unto you; as My Father hath sent Me, even so send I you. And when He had said this, He breathed on them and saith unto them: Receive ye the Holy Ghost. Whosoever sins ye remit, they are remitted unto them; and whosoever sins ye retain, they are retained. (John 20:21-23)

WHOM did the Father send? His only-begotten Son, "begotten of the Father before all worlds, God of God, Light of Light, very God of very God, begotten, not made, being of one substance with the Father" (Nicene Creed). Him God sent, Him who is holy, almighty, eternal, and infinite just as He is, the Son, by whom the world, together with the angels and men, was made and whose lordship at the same time is and remains also eternally obedient to the Father. The death of Him who was sent was not punishment, but sacrifice; and it did not happen because of His own guilt, but for the guilt of the world.

Whom does the Son send? Creatures who as such are essentially different from the Father and the Son, who as such had a beginning in time, who are limited and finite in every respect and still, despite their limitations, contend against Him to whom they owe everything. Disobedient, they rebel against the Father and the Son, their Creator and their Redeemer. The Son sends sinners, whose death is not a sacrifice but a consequence of sin and never a substitutionary death.

These contrasts notwithstanding, the commission of the risen Lord connects the Son and these men by the word "as," "as My Father hath sent Me, even so send I you."

What does the sending of the Son involve? The Father tore the Son from His heart. He sent Him who loves Him and with whom He is united in mutual love from eternity to eternity. Sending here means renunciation, surrender, sacrifice. In the mouth of Jesus the words "the Father hath sent Me" mean: The Father who loves Me became an angry Lord; the Father with whom I am one became another God, the God that forsook Me; the Father with whom I shared holiness made Me to be sin.

What does the Son's sending of men involve? It is not so much sending away as rather an urgent invitation, not so much a surrender as rather an enriching gift. In this sending God does not tear away from His heart, but draws to His heart. Those who are far from the heart of God are brought near when they are sent by the Son. "I, the Son, send you" means: I transform children of wrath into children of love, sinners into saints, men far off into men close to God. The Father who forsook you in anger is now your loving Father, who is always with you and who through you loves and invites others.

Although the sending of the Son and of men are thus in contrast, they are connected by the word "as" in the commission of the risen Lord.

The Son is sent by the Father, but the disciples are sent by the Son. Yet both the Son and the disciples are sent by God Himself. For the Son is in the Father, and the Father is in the Son. The word of the risen Lord, "As My Father hath sent Me, even so send I you," makes sinful men "ambassadors for Christ." Now this is true: "God did beseech you by us" (2 Cor. 5:20), as He besought through His Son. Sinful men are made apostles of Jesus Christ, messengers of God, and thereby brethren of Christ, the Apostle. (Heb. 3:1)

This fact no one can grasp. No one can fathom it. No one of himself can declare himself for it without committing the most grievous blasphemy. Only God Himself can make a man an apostle, can transform him, more, God must first create these men.

Christ does this by breathing on the disciples and saying to them, "Receive ye the Holy Ghost." Here the gesture accompanying the words is no less important than what He says. For the word which the evangelist uses to indicate this breathing is a very important word;

it is the same word used in the Greek Bible in the passage which declares that God breathed into the nostrils of the human form made of earth and thus created man a living soul (Gen. 2:7). The same word is used by the prophet Ezekiel when he speaks of the breath of God which clothed the dry bones with flesh and made them alive (Ezek. 37:5 ff.). This breath comes to the disciples as to dead men, indeed, to such as must first be created, as must first be made to be what they so evidently not yet are, messengers of the Son and with the Son messengers of the Father. In the sending of sinners as messengers of Jesus Christ nothing less is involved than in the creation of man at the beginning of the world. This sending is a creation and a resurrection of the dead.

To be sure, Christ had made these same men apostles already when He was on His way to meet the cross. There, too, He had sent them and promised them, "For it is not ye that speak, but the Spirit of your Father, which speaketh in you" (Matt. 10:20). Now, however, the risen Lord sends them again. And the unbelief and the denial of the disciples is not the only reason why they are sent again. No, they would not be the messengers of Jesus Christ if they were not sent both by Him who was to be crucified and by the risen Lord, by the Servant of God and the divine Lord. Thus they receive God's Spirit from the suffering and the risen Son. Only the Spirit who confesses Christ's death and resurrection is the Spirit of God.

The breath and the word of the risen Lord "Receive ye the Holy Ghost" does not make Pentecost small, but great. The gift of the Holy Ghost immediately after Jesus' resurrection and the outpouring of the Holy Ghost after the ascension of Jesus at Pentecost do not oppose but confirm each other. The reports of John's Gospel and of Acts are by their very duality extremely important and comforting. They give us the assurance that the reality of the Holy Spirit lies neither in the act of breathing nor in the rushing wind. But the Spirit who was given to the disciples by the risen Lord and was poured out on the company of believers on Pentecost is the eternal Spirit, who was before Pentecost and will be after Pentecost, who was before the creation of the world and will continue to act as Creator after it is gone. Not decisive is the question whether the risen Lord by His breathing merely made the disciples able to receive the coming Spirit (Chrysostom) or merely granted the disciples the gift to forgive sins (Jerome), whereas the fullness of the Spirit did not come upon the company of believers until Pentecost. What is decisive is this, that by the very number of Biblical testimonies the Holy Spirit is praised as the eternal Spirit who is never consumed in any actual gift of the Spirit, but is the Lord Himself. If the disciples, according to the command of the risen Lord, wait for the power of the Holy Ghost (Acts 1: 4, 8), they are really waiting for the Lord, who is the Spirit.

Thus God embraces men through the Son and the Holy Ghost and wrenches them out of their opposition to Him. They are seized by the Triune God, and now they are to be messengers in the name of the Triune God. He speaks to them through the Son and makes them over by the Holy Spirit, who proceeds from the Father and the Son. This is the work of the Holy Spirit: He creates confessors out of deniers, loving men out of loveless men, shepherds of the flock out of straying sheep. He makes sinners holy, the arrogant humble, the despairing confident, the wavering pillars and rocks. He makes them apostles of the one Apostle Jesus Christ, rocks of the one Cornerstone Jesus Christ, confessors of the only Confessor who did not fail, Jesus Christ. This means that the Holy Ghost makes sinful men to be images of the Son and thus images of God. For the Son "is the image of the invisible God." (Col. 1:15)

Therefore it follows: "Whosoever sins ye remit, they are remitted unto them; and whosoever sins ye retain, they are retained." You are not merely to offer God's forgiveness. You are not only to promise and hold out God's forgiveness as a prospect. You are not only to wish it to others and ask it for them. No, when you forgive, God Himself forgives. When you say, "Thy sins are forgiven thee," God Himself forgives. The word of forgiveness spoken by man is here "the voice of God coming down from heaven" (Melanchthon). To be sure, the Son alone "bears" all sins. The

101

disciples only proclaim men free from sins. But by their Word the Son makes them free.

In like manner retaining of sins is not only a warning, a threat, a reference to the future judgment. Much less is the retaining of sins only the unbelief of the people toward the word of forgiveness. But in place of the word of forgiveness Christ's messengers speak another word through which the guilt of the sinner is established, retained, preserved. Also in this word of men the Son Himself acts. When Jesus' messengers retain sins God retains them. No man can loose them, and God Himself does not loose them. "Whatsoever thou shalt bind on earth shall be bound in heaven; and whatsoever thou shalt loose on earth shall be loosed in heaven" (Matt. 16:19). As the word of Jesus "He that heareth you heareth Me" (Luke 10:16) applied to the messengers of Him who was then on the way to the cross, so it applies today to the messengers of the risen Lord. Whoever despises the messengers of Jesus Christ "treads Christ's blood underfoot." (Calvin)

To whom are sins to be forgiven? To whom are they to be retained?

The disciples are to forgive "as" Jesus Christ forgave. Beyond this the word of the risen Lord does not answer these questions. He says neither which sins nor whose sins are to be forgiven or retained. The disciples are simply to forgive as Jesus Christ forgave. But He did not forgive the small sins that He might retain the great, but He forgave the great sinners and passed the righteous by. Where sin has become great and alive, it is to be forgiven. "Sin that is felt, that torments me, that is alive, is called contrition" (Luther). However, Jesus Christ forgave not only where there was contrition, but His forgiveness was also so merciful that it produced contrition. Indeed, He forgave not only those who believed, but by His forgiveness He also invited men to believe and follow Him. As Jesus withdrew from the righteous and kept company with sinners, so the disciples are sent to those who are ablaze with their sins and are perishing.

The retaining of sins also demolishes the opinions of pious morality. Not simply the sins of those who did not amend their lives, where we have waited in vain for contrition and in whom we could see no evidence of true faith are to be retained. Sins are to be retained only to them to whom they have already been retained by God. Those are to be bound who are bound. The guilt is to be fixed for those to whom the Gospel has become "the savor of death unto death." (2 Cor. 2:16)

This twofold commission directs us beyond everything visible to our eyes, also beyond everything that church orders can fix — to the reality of the Holy Spirit, who knows what is in man and which men the Father has given to the Son. The decision concerning forgiveness and retention of sin is made not by man, neither by man speaking nor by man hearing, neither by his suffering under sin nor by his desiring forgiveness. This decision is made by God alone who knows His own in Christ and calls through the Word of His messengers.

A twofold word, then, has been given to the Church of Jesus Christ. The word of forgiveness is her primary commission. "For God sent not His Son into the world to condemn the world, but that the world through Him might be saved" (John 3:17). The disciples have no other mission. But aren't we again and again more concerned about retaining sins than about forgiving them? Isn't flagrant sin often more terrible to us than piety? How easy it is for us to preach repentance and how difficult to work repentance! To work repentance is so difficult because the loosing word of forgiveness is so difficult. Unlike all retaining of sins, this word of "forgiveness" is so difficult only because it is so unbelievably easy, because the grace of God is so inconceivably great and so unspeakably ready. In the last analysis, there is only one sin for the preacher and his people: not to believe forgiveness. "If you do not enter into the word 'sin is forgiven,' you enter into the word 'retained.'" (Luther)

The greeting of the risen Lord is, "Peace be unto you," not: Strife be unto you. Even though He sends them into a world without peace and home, peace is His greeting. Even though their message produces divisions, strife, and contention wherever they go, their greeting also is, Peace be unto you. Though their message makes alive and kills, it is, above all, the Word

104

of Life. As the commission to forgive sins is greater than the commission to retain sins, so peace is greater than disharmony, joy greater than fear, security greater than persecution. "Peace be with you" means: Peace will one day be yours, peace is yours now, and peace is given by you.

CHAPTER XV

The Seventh Word of the Risen Lord

And Jesus came and spake unto them, saying, All power is given unto Me in heaven and in earth. Go ye therefore, and teach all nations, baptizing them in the name of the Father and of the Son and of the Holy Ghost; teaching them to observe all things whatsoever I have commanded you. And, lo, I am with you alway, even unto the end of the world. Amen. (Matt. 28:18-20)

THE POWER to forgive sin is the greatest power on earth. Kings and mighty rulers long to free themselves and their companions from guilt by their own might, but they cannot, in spite of their might. The wealthy try to forget sin in their riches, artists in their art, and soldiers in their bravery. But they are all unable to free themselves or others of guilt. This power God has given only to His Son and to those whom the Son sends out, the apostles in their time and the messengers of the Word of God today. When the risen Lord breathed on His disciples, "Whosoever sins ye remit, they are remitted unto them," He gave power to them and their successors. "We also are lords and kings and have the greatest power, the power to rule."

"This power extends over all . . . no one is excepted, to all this lordship is announced and preached" (Luther). This great power appears as great weakness. What a disparity between the reality of the chosen disciples sent by the risen Lord and their power! Eleven men with no money, no weapons, no assistants, no knowledge of foreign languages — in fact, eleven men who at the moment are still in doubt about their commission are to rule over all nations! This disparity is so great that one is tempted to call those who accept this commission queer, if not mad. Only a government that feels very insecure can regard such men as dangerous. They are to rule, even if they have nothing to do with money, goods, sword, and force. All these are left for the lords of this world. "Our rule is aimed at another concern — sin. Where it moves, there our rule also moves; and where sin begins, there our rule moves in and begins to operate." "We are lords and kings, but this great power extends no farther than our sin." (Luther)

And yet the weakness of the disciples is no obstacle to their power. Their weakness and doubt are surrounded by the fourfold "all" that underlies their mission and makes them unconditionally victorious. This fourfold "all" in the saying of Jesus encloses the disciples like a wall and supports them like a rock. "All power," "all nations," "all commands," and "all the days" belong to the Lord, who sends out these disciples, and they have their unity in Him. On their ways the disciples cannot fall into strange hands without at once falling into the hands of the risen Lord, who embraces and holds them securely and who never leaves them. The fourfold "all" of this mission is held together by the one Christ, who speaks these words and who in them reveals the totality of His might. He is the Lord of heaven and earth, the Lord of the nations, the Lord of all authoritative words, and the Lord of all the days to the end of the world.

"All power is given unto Me in heaven and in earth." This is the authority for this mission. To His risen Son the Father has given power over the earth and the constellations, over every living thing on the earth, in and under the heavens, over all the living and the dead, over all human and subhuman creatures, and over the angels. To the risen Lord is given power over the good and the wicked, over the good angels and the devils, over the world as a good creation of God and over the world in its sinful and decadent form. The risen Lord rules not only His congregation but also the whole world, the good and the evil. Nothing is exempt from His rule. All things, everything, the Father has subjected to the risen Lord.

Thus also all nations are given to the risen Lord and are subjected to Him. Whether they know of Christ or not; whether they accept or reject this Lord; whether they put on a show of power or are weak;

whether they gather mighty forces or disintegrate and collapse — they are already under the power of Christ. They are all inescapably caught in the net that He will one day, at His return, draw up out of the river of history.

Together with all nations all governments, too, are subject to the risen Lord, whether they admit it or not. This is not denied by the fact that the risen Christ appeared only to women and disciples but not to Pontius Pilate and the high priest. We are not to conclude that neither a neutral nor a critical observer saw the risen Lord. No, the disciples and the women themselves had in the face of the cross all become critics and enemies of Christ as well as the priests and the Romans. Were they still true disciples when the risen Christ appeared to them, or did they not rather become disciples once more by His appearance? The risen Lord makes a disciple of him to whom He appears. He reveals Himself as the Victor before whom no despair and no stubbornness can persist.

But to the representatives of government He does not appear. For the risen Christ there is no longer a government to which He would be accountable. By ignoring it, He allows it to stand as the order of a fallen world, and with this fallen world it will come to its end. By not appearing to it, even though He had appeared to it before His death, He tells all who have ears to hear that He is no longer subject to government, but that, together with this world of sin and death, it has been placed at the free disposal of the risen Christ.

Thus Christ sends the disciples to conquered nations, who have not realized that they have been conquered. He sends them into a world of contradiction and great unrest. But this world is already in the firm possession of Christ. All the noise and fury of the world cannot change this fact, but only illuminate it.

This lordship Jesus Christ proclaims in His commandments. On His way from His baptism forward to the cross, and again from His resurrection to His ascension, He commanded all things that are necessary to know about Him here on earth. These commandments are the directive of the Lord to His subjects. These commandments are the manifest will of the one King, who in total authority meets every human individual. He has already given all His commandments. Now there remains "to observe all things, whatsoever I have commanded you."

The disciples therefore are to have no will and opinion of their own. They are simply to testify to what has already happened and to repeat what has already been said. They are not first to conquer, but they are to tell the conquered to whom they are subject and what their Conqueror demands of them. Thus the risen Lord sends out eleven weak people as heralds of His already accomplished victory and His already established might. Together with them we also should know that all the deeds for which we are sent out have already been done by Him. This, and this alone, is our victory: not our deeds, but testimony of His deed.

Thus the risen Christ sends out His disciples with the commission: "Go ye and make disciples of all nations." As He called sinners and made them His disciples, so these disciples are to call the nations and make disciples of them by Baptism and instruction. The command of Jesus says nothing about the sequence of Baptism and instruction, but He says: No Baptism without instruction — and no instruction without Baptism! By means of both the nations are to be delivered to the one Lord of all lords.

Now, as in every transfer to a lord, so in Baptism it is a matter of life and death. By Baptism the risen Lord takes over our life and death. But, unlike the lords of this world, He does not let us live in order to die for Him, but he lets us die in order that through Him we should live. Unlike the lords of this world, He does not want to take over our life to heighten His own, but He gives His life in order that thereby we come to have life. He wants our death. This means: He does not want us to die, but to receive His death as our possession. He wants our life for His own. This means: He wants to give us His life. His life should become our own, for He rose for us. Baptism is His assurance: I want you sinners in order to destroy your sin, which separates you from God. I want your death in order to abolish it, that you should live forever. This is the life that Baptism gives and works.

And as in every subordination to a lord, so also here knowledge and obedience are implied. But here it is an unconditional, perfect obedience, such as no sinner may demand of any other sinner. "All things whatsoever I have commanded you," you should "observe." All the words of Christ are to be preserved. All are to be followed. They are to be received as the last word. For His Word alone remains when all human words in their hollowness have collapsed.

In contradistinction to all the lords of this earth, for Christ to be a lord is to be a servant. He is the Lord as the Lamb that was slain for us. Unlike all the commands of earthly lords, the commands of Christ are a gift, His demands a presentation, His requirements a merciful offer. To obey Christ is to believe, to follow His precepts is to be filled with grace, to keep His commandments means to reveal oneself as one who is held and borne by Him. To be subject to the risen Lord is to become free; to follow Him is to stand beside Him; to obey Him is to be king with Him and with Him to rule the earth.

Thus the commandments of Christ that the disciples are to proclaim are good news (Mark 16:15). The Law of Christ, which the disciples and their successors are to lay upon the nations, is a gentle yoke and a very light burden. This is not force, but a most loving invitation: ". . . I will give you rest. Take My yoke upon you, and learn of Me." (Matt. 11:28 f.)

As the Triune God made the disciples to be repre-

112

sentatives and brothers of Jesus Christ, so they are to baptize the others in the name of the Triune God. As through the Son, who called them, and the Holy Ghost, who changed and created them, the disciples were delivered by the Triune God to the Triune God as His possession and instrument, so they are to baptize the others in the name of the Father and of the Son and of the Holy Ghost. God the Father and the Son and the Holy Ghost here have not three names, but one name. "It is one name, not several, and yet one word is not enough to name Him" (Schlatter). They are the one reality of the one God. As through God the Father and the Son and the Holy Ghost the disciples became the image of the Son and thus the image of God Himself, so in Baptism men of all times become brothers of, and heirs together with, Christ through the Holy Ghost, who proceeds from the Father and the Son. They become alive in the likeness of His life, they become sons as images of the only-begotten Son, they become glorious in the likeness of His glory, and as kings they reign through Him as He does. "Thereby they become the image of the Triune God. "Make disciples" means: Make sinners to be the image of God!

Although this is a mighty commission, it is disconcertingly easy. For all the work it demands has already been done. All the victories have been won. The crucified Christ's word, "It is finished!" includes all the ways and the words that the risen Lord commands His own. For time and eternity God has confirmed this

113

word from the cross by the resurrection of Jesus Christ from the dead. It can no longer be a question of conquering all nations, but only the revelation of this fact. The victory of Christ over all the world is no longer a question of fact, but only a question of time when this victory will be recognized by all the world. And even the time up to that moment is already enclosed by the lordship of Christ, just as the disciples were: "Lo, I am with you alway, even unto the end of the world."

This final "all" is not endless, like the "all" of "power in heaven and in earth," but it is limited, and this is our comfort. This final "all" is already finished by the victory of Christ, and every day and every hour until the revelation of this completion lies securely in His hand. He has enclosed the hours until He will turn time into eternity. "In all our work let us bear this in mind so that we keep before us not the existence but the end of the world. Then the Savior is with us all our days." "The Savior does not care to spend much effort on the existence of the world, because it is all so rotten anyway." (Chr. Blumhardt)

For all the days until the end this will hold: "Lo, I am with you." This is valid even though with this word the risen Lord leaves His disciples. He had appeared now here, now there; now here, now there, He had spoken and eaten with His own. Now those appearances are ended. But the risen Lord disappears only to be with His own all the more. He no longer

114

appears once here, once there, in order that He might be among them everywhere and always. Thus His absence between the ascension and the return is a greater presence. In fact, though it sounds like a paradox, the ascending Christ comes to His congregation and is more present and more at hand than was the risen Christ during the forty days. Now no one need wait until the risen Lord appears to Him, for He is constantly and everywhere among those who call on Him and praise His name. But if this fellowship between Him and His own even now is so complete, what will it be when at His return He puts an end to this world and we shall see Him!

CHAPTER XVI

The Eighth Word of the Risen Lord

And He said unto them: Go ye into all the world, and preach the Gospel to every creature. He that believeth and is baptized shall be saved; but he that believeth not shall be damned. And these signs shall follow them that believe: In My name shall they cast out devils; they shall speak with new tongues; they shall take up serpents; and if they drink any deadly thing, it shall not hurt them; they shall lay hands on the sick, and they shall recover. (Mark 16:15-18)

SOMEDAY the exalted Lord will return, to judge the living and the dead. He will appear in His glory and visibly establish His dominion upon earth. "Then shall all the tribes of the earth mourn" (Matt. 24:30). Then every man must appear before the throne of Christ and give account for every word and every deed. Then men of all the ages will receive their verdict from His mouth.

This decision of the Last Judgment is taking place even now. The final verdict is being given already today, in the time between the ascension and the return of Christ — in the preaching of the Gospel.

116

"He that believeth and is baptized shall be saved."
This means: He shall be acquitted when Christ comes
to judge the world. He who is baptized is safely sheltered in Christ's death and resurrection. For him who
believes, his own deeds and words are covered with the
deed and Word of Christ, which God imputes to him,
the sinner. The work of Christ is so much the believer's
own that he may óne day present it in the Judgment
as his own God-pleasing work. Who can condemn him
then?

"But he that believeth not, shall be damned." He
shall be condemned, bound, and delivered to eternal
death on the Day of Judgment. For him who does not
believe, for him even his Baptism will be of no value.

As man is confronted with the preaching of the
Gospel, the last Judgment is taking place already now.
For in the preaching by the church the voice of the
Christ who has come sounds forth. In fact, already in
the Gospel the voice of the Christ who shall come
again calls out: "He that believeth on Him is not
condemned; but he that believeth not is condemned
already, because he hath not believed in the name of
the only-begotten Son of God."

The decision of the Last Judgment is at one and
the same time the decision for eternal life or eternal
death, the decision of resurrection to life or to death.
Thus the preaching of the Gospel coincides with the
dawn of the new creation even now in the midst of
this world. "The hour is coming, and now is, when

117

the dead shall hear the voice of the Son of God, and they that hear shall live" (John 5:25). Whoever believes the Gospel already has eternal life and does not merely expect to receive it. Whoever is baptized, is already risen with Christ (Col. 2:13; 3:1). He is not only approaching the resurrection. The believer is even now a "new creature." "Old things are passed away; behold, all things are become new." (2 Cor. 5:17)

The creation, and this means the new creation, is the focal point of the word which the Gospel of St. Mark records as the last word of the risen Christ. He commands not only: Preach the Gospel to all nations, to all sinners, to all who repent; indeed, He orders not only: Preach the Gospel to all men — but also preach it "to every creature," to the whole creation. "This word does not indicate that it is to be preached to mankind alone, but that it should be proclaimed before all creatures so that there is no corner on earth where it must not be heard before the Last Day." "To every creature, this means: Nothing is excluded, whatever it may be: emperors, kings, princes, sun, moon, fish, animals. . . ." The Gospel is to be preached to every creature, "so that even the sun and the moon hear it. It is not to be a limited preaching, like the Law of Moses." (Luther)

Actually, the Gospel is for all creatures: to be sure, "for men, first of all, and, secondly, for the other creatures" (Bengel), but surely also for the other creatures. For the whole creation groans and moans with us,

118

waiting for the revelation of the children of God and for the deliverance from the powers and curse of its futility. The Gospel begets the children of God and reveals them to the world as a new creature and as the glory of God the Creator, even when the community of these children is afflicted and seems to be consigned to a constant dying. Thus the preaching of the Gospel is itself already the dawn of the new creature, and preachers of the Gospel are sent for the service of creation, namely, of this, the new creation. In preaching and in the Sacraments it violently bursts upon the old world. It is more real than the visible reality of this old world. In spite of its invisibility it is more beautiful than all the glory of this aging world. Only the new creation is free, for it serves God and is no longer subject to the devil as its master. The preachers of the Gospel are the servants of the new man, the new heaven, the new earth, the heavenly Jerusalem, for they testify of the resurrection. But if Christ is risen, by whom all things are made, how should we not also rise with Him as a new creation, for we have been made by Him, and our sins have been atoned for by His death?

Thus the signs that follow the believers are the foretokens of the new creature, the foretokens of the new man, the new heaven and the new earth, which the returning Christ will visibly establish in the place of the world that has passed away.

"And these signs shall follow them that believe:

In My name shall they cast out devils." The devil, the lord of this world, the god of those who live in the captivity of sin, is the highest one to whom the sinner can rise in his own power. He is the slaveholder of sinners and gives them neither truth nor life. He possesses men by belying them, making them sick, and taking their life. He possesses all the world, since by sin it has been put under his power. This devil the returning Christ will bind and cast into the bottomless pit for all eternity. But even now his power is to be broken by the name of Christ, which the believers confess before the devil-tormented creatures. By the mouth of His congregation the Lordship of the Christ replaces the devil as master of the world. Before it the devil must even now give place.

"They shall speak with new tongues." The confusion of languages, to which God once consigned the arrogant nations of this earth, will someday come to an end. The confusion of unintelligibility, in which people speak against one another in an insane attempt "to make themselves a name" (Gen. 11:4), will someday be removed by the song of the redeemed as they come out of all nations before the throne of God and unite with one voice to worship the Lamb slain for the world. Then "every creature which is in heaven and on the earth and under the earth and such as are in the sea, and all that are in them" will cry with one accord: "Blessing, and honor, and glory, and power be unto Him that sitteth upon the throne and unto the

Lamb forever and ever" (Rev. 5:13). This song is beginning even now in the midst of the corrupt world wherever the Holy Ghost creates new tongues to praise the works of God and new ears to hear this song.

"They shall take up serpents" — that creature that from the very beginning was the tool and symbol of the adversary and in bitter enmity would bruise man's heel (Gen. 3:15). The destructive power and the venomous hostility of the serpent has for the believer already been ended. If it now fastens itself on him, it is to be grasped, shaken off, and driven away in faith; it will do no harm (Acts 28:3-6). In fact, the believer may play with serpents, may take them in his hand as peaceful and harmless creatures. For the believer, who himself is a foretoken of the coming Lord, waits under these foretokens for the coming time, when wolves and lambs shall dwell together, when lions and cattle shall feed together, and when children shall lead calves and lions as one flock. (Is. 11:6 f.)

"And if they drink any deadly thing, it shall not hurt them." As a sign of the future eternal life, the life of the believers is already now wonderfully protected and preserved. "They shall lay hands on the sick, and they shall recover." As a sign of the future eternal life the believers may in the name of Jesus prolong and preserve the life of others. "The prayer of faith shall save the sick, and the Lord shall raise him up" (James 5:15). Life that is thus prolonged is not eternal life but a foretoken of eternal life. The body that is thus preserved is not the spiritual body of one raised from the dead but a sign of it, just as the resurrection of Lazarus by the command of Christ was not yet the resurrection to eternal life but a sign of that future resurrection.

These are the signs that shall follow them that believe. The risen Christ does not say that they shall follow every one of the believers. But "the believers," the congregation of Jesus Christ in its faith in the exalted Lord, shall never be without such signs.

Let us not excuse ourselves from the promise and the claim of these words as in our self-appointed modesty we restrict them to the apostles and the first Christian congregation: "These miracles were necessary at the beginning of the Church. In order that the faith of the Christians might take root, it was necessary to fortify it by miracles, just as we also, when planting trees, water them until they are rooted in the ground and then quit watering them" (Gregory). No, the promise is given without limitation. In general, and not only to the apostles, Jesus said: "He that believeth on Me, the works that I do, he shall do also; and greater works than these shall he do." (John 14:12)

Nor should we deny these promises by "spiritualizing" them: "All believers speak with new tongues when they forsake the language of the world . . .; they take up serpents when by wholesome admonition they take sin from the heart; they drink poison without harm when they hear poisonous temptations but do not let

122

themselves be misled to wicked works" (Gregory). No, to spiritualize these promises is to void them! Here it does not apply that "the more spiritual the miracles, the greater they are," and that they are greatest "by which not bodies but souls are raised" (Gregory). The Spirit that is at work in the church is the creating Spirit which creates new bodies in the resurrection. The physically risen Lord directs His promises also to the physical life.

Neither fear of the unusual nor recognition of personal weakness of faith should keep the congregation of today from reckoning with signs and wonders. At no time should the Church of Jesus Christ be without those who in faith dare lay their hands upon the sick for healing and dare command devils to come out of those who are possessed. If only everyone would not always pray only that God Himself would grant him help and healing! If we could only believe that for each other! If only we would believe that in the name of Jesus the Creator of all things, together with His omnipotence and holiness, has become our Friend, our very own! The believing congregation may at all times press onward through deadly attacks in the confident knowledge that they can harm her neither physically nor spiritually.

But what if, in spite of such signs, the attacks of the devil increase? What if the devil really rages and practically destroys the congregation in spite of the fact that within it victories over him are gained? What if in spite of such signs the sufferings increase and the believers are delivered into death even if they believe the promise? What are we to think when one believer miraculously stays alive and another is sent to his death? What are we to think when the risen Christ Himself commanded Peter to suffer and die and destined John to survive and to live? What are we to think when Peter's hands were stretched out on the arm of the cross and he died, while, according to an ancient legend, the poison that was given John to drink did not harm him?

The risen Christ replies: "If I will that he tarry till I come, what is that to thee?" (John 21:22). If the one lives — what is that to you? If only he lives unto the Lord and in faith hastens toward His return! If another dies — what is that to you? If only he dies unto the Lord and in faith follows His death! If the one lives — what is that to you? Die unto your Lord and follow Him! If another dies — what is that to you? Live unto the Lord and go to meet Him! If only we are in the Lord and by our faith praise Him!

"So then after the Lord had spoken unto them, He was received up into heaven, and sat on the right hand of God." (Mark 16:19)

CHAPTER XVII

Praise and Petition

Christ is arisen from the grave's dark prison.
We now rejoice with gladness; Christ will end all
sadness.
Lord, have mercy.

All our hopes were ended had Jesus not ascended
From the grave triumphantly. For this, Lord Christ,
we worship Thee.
Lord, have mercy.

Hallelujah! Hallelujah! Hallelujah!
We now rejoice with gladness; Christ will end all
sadness.
Lord, have mercy.

Christ to heav'n arose. What did He send to us below?
The Paraclete, the Holy Ghost, to comfort all the
Christian host.
Hallelujah.

Hallelujah! Hallelujah! Hallelujah!
We now rejoice with gladness; Christ will end all
   sadness.
Lord, have mercy.

Lord Jesus Christ, Thou Son of the Living God! As
after Thy joyful resurrection Thou didst visit Thy sorrowing disciples, to comfort them and give them gladness, we heartily beseech Thee to appear unto us and
all Christendom with Thy peace and joy.

Give peace to our heart. Grant peace to our land, and
then let us eternally rejoice in the mansions of peace.

O Lord, show unto us and all sorrowing souls Thy
wounds, that in the face of all enemies we may be
glad in Thy suffering and Thy joyful resurrection.

Give us the Holy Spirit, that we may daily rise from
the death of sin and walk in a new life.

Thou blessed King of Easter, let our bodies be like
unto Thy glorified body on that Day.

Keep us all in the sincere joy of Easter, and then grant
unto us all the peace of the eternal Easter, Thou who,
with the Father and the Holy Ghost, art blessed to all
eternity! Amen.